The Henry L. Stimson Lectures Series

Yale

UNIVERSITY PRESS

NEW HAVEN & LONDON

The Paradox of Liberation

Secular Revolutions and Religious Counterrevolutions

Michael Walzer

The Henry L. Stimson Lectures at the Whitney and Betty
MacMillan Center for International and Area Studies at Yale.

Yale University Press books may be purchased in quantity for educational, business, or promotional use. For information, please e-mail
sales.press@yale.edu (U.S. office) or sales@yaleup.co.uk (U.K. office).

Set in Janson type by Integrated Publishing Solutions,
Grand Rapids, Michigan.
Printed in the United States of America.

Library of Congress Control Number 2014031910
ISBN 978-0-300-18780-9 (cloth : alk. paper)

A catalogue record for this book is available from the British Library.

This paper meets the requirements of ANSI/NISO Z39.48–1992
(Permanence of Paper).

10 9 8 7 6 5 4 3 2 1

To the memory of Clifford Geertz (1926–2006)
colleague and friend
who would have argued with me about this book

Contents

vii

Contents

Preface

My project in this book is to describe a recurrent and, to my mind, disturbing pattern in the history of national liberation. I will discuss a small set of cases: the creation of three independent states in the years after World War II—India and Israel in 1947–48 and Algeria in 1962—and I will focus on the secular political movements that achieved statehood and the religious movements that challenged the achievement roughly a quarter century later. In the first chapter, I will refer to all three liberation movements—the Indian National Congress, Labor Zionism, and the Algerian FLN (National Liberation Front), but chiefly to the FLN. I will also refer, because I have written about it and because it has been a general reference for Western writers about revolution and national liberation, to the exodus of the ancient Israelites from Egypt, which is arguably the earliest example, in literature if not in history, of the liberation of a nation from foreign rule. In the second chapter, I will examine the recurrent pattern in detail in the case I know best, the Zionist movement and the state it created. In chapter 3, I will consider an alternative view of all three cases, defended primarily by Marxist writers. And in the fourth chapter, I will take up a second alternative view, developed by Indian writers in postcolonial studies, and then ask whether national liberation has a future, looking first and most extensively at India and then, again, at Israel.

I won't pretend that the pattern I am going to describe is universal or that it is precisely the same in all its iterations. I follow the maxim about political life that nothing is the same as anything else, but that some things—events, processes, movements, and regimes—are similar to other things, and careful comparisons can help us understand the similarities and the differences. Friends and colleagues whom I consulted about my project worried about the extent of the differences and called my attention to this or that outlying case. In India, for example, I was told very emphatically that Algeria was the outlier because of the authoritarian character of the state the FLN established— and I have adopted something like that position here. A number of colleagues and early readers argued that the Zionists are the outliers because of the Jewish exile and the initial and ongoing struggle with the Palestinian Arabs. I mean to deal with those issues, but my primary subject is national liberation itself and what I will call, for the moment, its internal relations. Here, as readers will see, the similarities across the three cases are very strong.

It is important to stress that my aim throughout is understanding, not scientific explanation. I make no claim that the three case pattern can be expressed as a set of covering laws; there are historical and contemporary cases that the "laws" wouldn't cover. Indeed, these three can each be described in ways that would greatly complicate my schematic account. I will supply some of the complications after laying out the general scheme. But I believe that my account, even in its simplest version, provides a useful beginning for a necessary inquiry: What happened to national liberation?

Initially, at least, this is a success story: the three nations were indeed liberated from foreign rule. At the same time, however, the states that now exist are not the states envisioned by the original leaders and intellectuals of the national liberation movements, and the moral/political culture of these states, their inner life, so to speak, is not at all what their founders expected. One difference is central to my analysis, and I will keep coming back to it: all three movements were secular, committed, indeed, to an explicitly secular project, and yet in the states that they created a politics rooted in what we can loosely call fundamentalist religion is today very powerful. In three different countries, with three different religions, the timetable was remarkably similar: roughly twenty to thirty years after independence, the secular state was challenged by a militant religious movement. This unexpected outcome is a central feature of the paradox of national liberation.

The same story could be told with other cases and other timetables. Two very different versions of secular politics made their appearance in the twentieth century. The first version was openly authoritarian: Lenin in Russia and Atatürk in Turkey are its primary representatives; Nasser in Egypt and the Baath parties in Syria and Iraq are later examples of authoritarian secularism. The Algerian FLN could be included in this group; the state that it established immediately after independence allowed only one political party, and even that party was soon taken over by the army it supposedly controlled. But since the FLN was, at the beginning, formally committed to democracy, and since at least some of its militants sustained that commitment, I have chosen to link it with the more consistently democratic examples of India and Israel. The combination of democratic and secularist commitments is, to my mind, critically important to the project of national liberation; it is the key reason for calling the movements I will be discussing "liberationist." Or, better, it is my reason for distinguishing them from other revolutionary and nationalist movements, even though some of these others have also been challenged, down the road, by a religious counterrevolution.

All three of the national liberation movements considered here have been attacked as "Westernizing" by their religious (and also by their postcolonial) critics. The charge is undoubtedly true. In important ways, the liberationists imitate the politics of the European left. Since that is the source of my own politics, the criticism doesn't particularly bother me. But it points to another aspect of the paradox of national liberation: the militants go to school with the very people whose imperial rule they are fighting, and they have a view of their own nation that is remarkably close to what Edward Said called "orientalism." That term, like "Westernizing," is meant to be pejorative, and yet there is much to be said in favor of the "orientalists"—and some things also to be said against them. The problematic connection of the national liberation militants to the nation they aim to liberate is central to my argument in the chapters that follow. This is the "internal relation" that I mean to examine; it goes a long way toward explaining the religious counterrevolution.

My first question—What happened to national liberation?—points us toward another: What happened to the secular democratic left? Here is the deeper question—perhaps I should call it the anxiety—that led me to write this book. It is a question that transcends my three cases, but I don't want to write about it in abstraction. I have always had difficulty sustaining an abstract argument for more than a few sentences. I want to write concretely, and India, Israel, and Algeria provide useful examples of the secular left's difficulties with political hegemony and cultural reproduction. There are other possibly illustrative cases. I could even discuss these difficulties with reference to the United States, whose revolution wasn't a national liberation struggle, although it provides an impressive example of secular (and at least quasi-democratic) commitment. Readers who doubt that there has ever been a significant secular left in this country should take a look at our earliest history. The first settlers and the political founders freed themselves or, better, began to free themselves, from the religious establishments of the Old World, and they set up what I think is the first secular state in world history. In a brief postscript, I will explain why the paradox that marks the twentieth-century cases is absent in eighteenth-century America. This is an argument for American exceptionalism, which I will make with one important qualification. However exceptional Americans were in the eighteenth century, we are less exceptional today.

The Paradox of Liberation

ONE

The Paradox of National Liberation

I

National liberation is an ambitious and also, from the beginning, an ambiguous project. The nation has to be liberated not only from external oppressors—in a way, that's the easy part—but also from the internal effects of external oppression. Albert Memmi, the Tunisian Jew who wrote perceptively about the psychological effects of foreign rule, makes the critical point. The Jews will have to be delivered from "a double oppression: an objective external oppression made up of the . . . incessant aggressions inflicted on [them] *and* an auto-oppression . . . whose consequences were just as harmful."[1] One of the consequences of these two together is the internal domination of traditional elites, the mediators of foreign rule—the men and women, mostly men, who move back and forth between the subject nation and its rulers, negotiating with the rulers, bribing them when necessary, accommodating their demands when that seems necessary, making the best of a difficult and often humiliating relationship. The figure of the "court Jew" has parallels in every nation ruled by foreigners, and one of the aims of national liberation is the elimination of this role and the defeat of the people who made it their own.

But another, even more important effect of this doubled oppression has to be overcome, and that is the passivity, the quietude, the deep lethargy of the dominated people. No nation can live for long under foreign rule, or, like the Jews, in exile, without accommodating to its condition and making its peace with the powers that be. Early attempts at resistance are repressed, often brutally; after that, resistance goes underground, where it finds expression in common complaint, mockery, and evasion. Leftist scholars have contrived to celebrate this sort of thing, and it ought to be celebrated.[2] But the larger, sadder story is one of accommodation, the practical alternatives generally being less attractive. Accommodation will be more or less profound depending on the severity of the conditions that have to be accommodated and the number of years, or decades, or centuries during which those conditions prevail. In the sphere of politics, accommodation takes a variety of forms: fatalistic resignation, withdrawal from political activity to familial or communal concerns, even acceptance of the political "superiority" of the foreign rulers. In this last case, the local culture is reconceived as somehow unsuited to politics, devoted to higher, more spiritual pursuits. "They," the British, the French, Europeans generally, have a talent for politics; they have the ruthlessness necessary for imperial domination; "we" submit because we are focused on more important things; ruthlessness is alien to us.[3]

Even liberationists like Mohandas Gandhi, who didn't want to imitate the ruthlessness of imperial rulers, believed nonetheless that the old accommodation had to be overcome; it was necessary to "train the masses in self-consciousness and the attainment of power." Gandhi's "constructive program" was aimed at producing men and women who were "fit" for independence, capable of "managing [their] own affairs"—though not, like the British, everyone else's.[4] This task should rightly have preceded national liberation but was, in all my cases, unfinished at the moment when independence was won. From the beginning the constructive programs of the liberationists met with difficulties.

Once people have settled in and adjusted themselves, one way or another, to a particular version of foreign rule, the men and women who suddenly appear and offer to liberate them are likely to be regarded with suspicion—as Moses was when he tried to explain to the Israelites that they were about to be delivered from Egyptian slavery.[5] Here the biblical text tells a classic story, which is repeated again and again when young and enthusiastic liberators first encounter the people they mean to liberate and find them frightened and reluctant. The liberators soon discover that they need (in modern terms) to "raise the consciousness" of the people before liberation is possible.

What can this mean except to oppose the people's already existing consciousness, which has been shaped by oppression and accommodation? Raising consciousness is a persuasive enterprise, but it quickly turns into a cultural war between the liberators and what we can call the traditionalists. Raising consciousness can be a tense business. It's possible for a charismatic leader like Gandhi to adapt the traditional culture to the needs of national liberation, but adaptations along these lines are likely to face fierce opposition; their success may well be brief. And even Gandhi was deeply opposed to many aspects of Hindu culture, especially the fate of the "untouchables." He was assassinated by someone committed to a more literal, or more traditional, or perhaps more radically nationalist version of Hinduism.[6]

I have taken this example, and all my examples, from the history of nationalism, but I want to stress that national liberation is a subset of that history, a piece of it, not the whole of it. Indeed, the liberationist project seems somewhat at odds with Webster's definition of nationalism: "a sense of national consciousness exalting one nation above all others and placing primary emphasis on promotion of its culture and interests as opposed to those of other nations."[7] There are certainly men and women with this sort of consciousness in all the national liberation movements —they form its right wing. Nationalism for them is a zerosum game. But the "primary emphasis" of the movements' leaders is doubly different: first, they aim to achieve political equality with, rather than a dominant position over, other nations, and, second, they aim to liberate their own nation from long-standing traditions of authoritarianism and passivity—indeed, from its own historic culture. Liberation is closer to revolutionary politics than to national aggrandizement. Like the liberationist militants, revolutionaries set themselves in opposition to established patterns of submission, accommodation, and (what Marxists call) "false consciousness." They aim at a radical transformation. Social revolution requires a struggle against the existing society; national liberation requires a struggle against, rather than an "exaltation" of, the existing nation.

This is also, often, an antireligious struggle, for religion, as Jawaharlal Nehru wrote, teaches "a philosophy of submission . . . to the prevailing social order and to everything that is."[8] Nehru was repeating here the standard liberationist view, which follows from the fact that accommodation to foreign rule commonly takes a religious form—in part for the obvious reason that otherworldliness offers comforts that are always available, however bad things are here and now. But the secular militants of national liberation are mistaken if they describe the comforts of religion as nothing more than pie in the sky. Religion also generates fantasies of reversal and triumph and then, intermittently, revivalist and millenarian movements that are sometimes tumultuous but always ineffective.[9] Millenarianism looks like opposition to foreign rule, and may be that briefly, but over the long run it is a form of political accommodation—for it doesn't produce a steady or persistent oppositional politics, and the millennium never arrives. Another, more concrete form of accommodation is resolutely this-worldly and doesn't look forward to apocalyptic events. In fact, most religions prescribe a regimen that can and should be established right now. It requires submission from ordinary believers and assigns an authoritative role to traditional religious leaders—who are often already local officials and judges, appointed by and submissive in turn to foreign rulers.

But neither millenarian nor traditionalist politics invites ideological commitment or long-term activism. Nor does either politics promise individual freedom, political independence, citizenship, democratic government, scientific education, or economic advance. It is for the sake of all these that the national liberationist or revolutionary militants need to transform the people in whose name they are acting—and that transformation requires the defeat of the people's religious leaders and the overcoming of the people's customary way of life. V. S. Naipaul, writing thirty years after Indian national liberation, perfectly captures the attitude of the liberators toward the religion of the people:

> Hinduism . . . has exposed us to a thousand years of defeat and stagnation. It has given men no idea of a contract with other men, no idea of a state. It has enslaved one quarter of the population and always left the whole fragmented and vulnerable. Its philosophy of withdrawal has diminished men intellectually and not equipped them to respond to challenge; it has stifled growth.[10]

National liberation, by contrast, is a secularizing, modernizing, and developmental creed. It is, as its opponents say, a "Western" creed, and to the nation about to be liberated, it is something entirely new. Indeed, newness is the mantra of the liberators. They offer the oppressed people a new beginning, a new politics, a new culture, a new economy; they aim to create new men and women. Thus David Ben-Gurion: "The worker of Eretz Yisrael [the Land of Israel] differs from the Jewish worker in Galut [exile] . . . [He is] not a new branch grafted to an old tradition, but a new tree"—literally, in Ben-Gurion's eyes, a new kind of Jew.[11] Similarly, Frantz Fanon: "There is a new kind of Algerian man. The power of the Algerian Revolution . . . resides in the radical mutation that the Algerian has undergone."[12]

We can gain some sense of what all this means from the history of the United States: what Ralph Waldo Emerson and his contemporaries called "the American newness" was achieved through the escape from Old World tyrannies and traditions. In American history, as in the history of ancient Israel, the victory of the new required a geographic move rather than a political movement. Indeed, the American experience led Louis Hartz to argue that the "only really successful revolution is . . . a migration."[13] But the same sense of starting over is present in all the cases of national liberation, even if the new beginning is in an old place.

Of course, this newness encounters resistance, which begins as a stubborn allegiance to the-way-things-have-always-been but soon becomes ideological and therefore also new: fundamentalism and ultra-Orthodoxy are both modernist reactions to attempts at modernist transformation. The slogan of Jewish ultra-Orthodoxy, "Everything new is forbidden by the Torah," is itself a new idea; it would have made the historic accommodation to exile impossible.[14] Jewish survival required a lively adaptability and a readiness for innovation. But the slogan works well against attempts to bring the exile to an end, and one can find similar examples of opposition to the newness of national liberation in India and Algeria. What is more surprising is the reappearance of this opposition after the achievement of political independence, when the defenders of traditional religion, themselves renewed and modernized, begin the construction of a counterrevolutionary politics.

I had better tell a particular story now or at least provide a brief example of what I am talking about, to avoid too schematic an account. I will begin with the Algerian case because it is in several ways the outlier among my three. First of all, French repression in Algeria was more brutal than that of the English in either India or Palestine, and it was mirrored in the brutality of the National Liberation Front's internal wars, in the FLN's terrorist campaign against European settlers (advocates of terrorism were marginal in India and a small minority among the Zionists), and also in the FLN's postindependence authoritarianism. Second, the commitment to secular liberation in Algeria, although it finds an avid spokesman in Frantz Fanon, was probably weaker than in my other cases. The most visible leaders of the FLN were indeed secular and Marxist, or at least socialist, in their political commitment. But the movement's initial manifesto, read over Cairo radio in 1954, called for an "Algerian state, sovereign, democratic, and social, within the framework of the principles of Islam."[15] There were people in the FLN who took this framework seriously—and who demanded immediately after independence that it be put in place. In the early years, however, FLN militants displayed little interest in Islamic principles, and the Soummam Platform of 1956, the work primarily of the internal FLN and its Berber leaders, actually left the principles of Islam out of its description of the movement's goal: "the birth of an Algerian state in the form of a democratic and social republic—and not the restoration of monarchy or of a theocracy." In Cairo a year later, a compromise was reached with a new text that called for "the establishment of a democratic and social Algerian republic, which is not in contradiction with the principles of Islam."[16]

In any case, the leaders of the FLN did not spend much time learning about the principles of Islam. Sitting in a French prison, Ahmed Ben Bella, the future first president of Algeria, read the leftist publications of the Paris publisher Maspero and studied the works of Lenin, Sartre, and Malraux. In the aftermath of independence, he argued for something he called "Islamic socialism," which was, as his Muslim critics claimed, more socialist than Islamic. His chief advisors as president were Trotskyists. Ramdane Abane, one of the FLN's leading intellectuals and a defender of terrorism, spent five years in prison (1950–55), where he "applied himself to a voracious reading of revolutionary studies, Marx and Lenin—and even *Mein Kampf*." He had already gained his *baccalauréat;* he must have done all his reading in French. Many of the FLN militants, and a larger number of the intellectuals, were Francophone. The establishment of the Provisional Government of the Republic of Algeria was announced in French by Ferhat Abbas, then the head of the FLN.[17] The FLNers were certainly committed Algerian nationalists: "It's not with you but against you that we are learning your language," declares a character in a novel by an Algerian writer (who wrote in French).[18] At the same time, many of these nationalists were culturally Francophile or, perhaps better, Europhile: Hocine Ait Ahmed—a Berber and, along with Ben Bella, one of the *"neuf historiques,"* the Historic Nine, founders of the FLN—concentrated in his prison years on English literature. Although militants like Ben Bella and Ait Ahmed aimed at ending foreign rule, they were remarkably at ease in a foreign culture.

Important Muslim scholars, organized in the Association of Algerian Ulama, condemned the eager reception of European culture by many Algerians, especially in the cities, and demanded the exclusive use of Arabic in Algerian schools. The association foreshadowed the Islamic revival of the 1980s and 1990s—whose militants fiercely opposed the bilingualism advocated by Mostefa Lacheraf, an old FLNer who was cultural affairs minister in the late 1970s. As Cliffort Geertz writes about similar reformist groups in Morocco, "These were *oppositional* Muslims . . . Into what had been a fine medieval contempt for infidels crept a tense modern note of anxious envy and defensive pride."[19] But the ulama were unable to produce a modern nationalist politics, and they were opposed in turn by Muslim "moderates." The moderates urged the French to allow the imposition of Islamic family law and to make many lesser concessions to Muslim sensitivities but, given that, had no further difficulty with French rule. Muslim officials in Algeria were fully engaged in the politics of subservience; the Soummam Platform contemptuously described them as "domesticated, chosen and paid by the colonial administration." These officials were the more immediate opponents of the FLN militants, whose political agenda included, as the writings of Fanon make clear, not only ending French rule but also overcoming the colonial mentality and the Algerian past.[20]

FLN radicalism helps explain the highly visible role that women were given in the movement, not in the leadership—an absence that signaled things to come—but on the ground, in military (and terrorist) activities. Compare the role of women among Zionist militants, especially in the Haganah, the military arm of the Zionist movement. (The Indian National Congress had no military arm, but for the sake of symmetry, let me note Nehru's boast that Congress's political and social movements "have drawn tens of thousands of middle-class women into . . . public activity" for the first time.)[21] Putting women forward in the FLN was not an affront to the French oppressors; it was directed against the internal oppression of Algeria's religious tradition. Fanon, in his portentous way, makes this a central theme: "The militant man discovers the militant woman, and jointly they create new dimensions for Algerian society." And again: "The freedom of the Algerian people . . . [is now] identified with woman's liberation, with her entry into history." And again: "[In the movement] the woman ceased to be a mere complement of the man. Indeed, it might be said that she pulled up her roots through her own exertions."[22]

This uprooting succeeded brilliantly for a time but, as contemporary Algerian politics attests, it ultimately failed. "Alas," Alistair Horne wrote in his 1977 history of the Algerian war, "the promissory notes issued [to women] in the heat of battle have yet to be fully honored."[23] Now it seems fair to say that they have hardly been honored at all. Although the political standing of Islam in Algeria today is contested, its cultural authority is unquestionably greater than FLN militants would have predicted it would be after fifty years of "liberation." And the social standing of women in Algeria today, though also contested, is far short of the equality that the same militants promised their "sisters" in the 1950s. The FLN was a revolution in the making; resurgent Islam is the counterrevolution.

Truth to tell, the retreat from revolutionary feminism began soon after the FLN victory in 1962, as Horne suggests, and it was confirmed in the Family Code adopted in 1984, despite the fierce opposition of many female veterans of the liberation struggle—including Djamila Bouhired, who had been captured and tortured by the French after trying to plant a bomb in a café during the Battle of Algiers. She was a hero of the liberation struggle (for the record: not one of my heroes), but she was not a political force in the post-liberation FLN. The new law made it a legal duty for Algerian women to obey their husbands, institutionalized polygamy, and denied wives the right to apply for a divorce unless they gave up all claims to alimony.[24] Still, the Islamist zealots who terrorized Algeria in the 1990s demanded many more restrictions on the everyday lives of women—on dress, mobility, and employment.

Imam Ali Belhadj, a founder and leader of the Islamic Salvation Front (FIS), has called for the seclusion of women in the home, which they should not leave "except under conditions provided by law." In an article published in 2003, Zahia Smail Salhi writes, "Harassment has been relentless and unbearable, particularly for women who live alone or who refuse to wear the veil in the workplace." One FIS tract warns women against using "the Jewish word 'emancipation' to attack the Islamic values of your ancestors."[25] The writer may have forgotten that emancipation was a central concept of the early FLN radicals.

Emancipation was central also to the program of Indian national liberation, where it required a direct attack on the religious culture and social practices of both Hindus and Muslims. When the Indian Constitution was being debated, Rajkumari Amrit Kaur, one of the founders of the All India Women's Conference, urged the drafting committee to make sure that the religious liberty clause allowed the "wiping out" of religiously sanctified "evils" like purdah, child marriage, polygamy, unequal laws of inheritance, the ban on intercaste marriage, and the dedication of girls to temples.[26] Kaur, who became the minister of health in Nehru's first cabinet, had been educated at the Sherborne School for Girls in Dorset and at Oxford University. She was in many ways a modern Western woman and at the same time an Indian nationalist and an early feminist. Needless to say, the evils were not immediately wiped out, although the new civil code for Hindus, adopted in the 1950s, made many of them illegal.

A Francophone and even a Francophile Algerian militant was not unusual. Similarly, the organizations that came together in 1885 to create the Indian National Congress were dominated by Anglophone and Anglophile lawyers, journalists, and officials. The architects of liberation have a lot in common with the architects of oppression (who produced, according to Marx's famous articles on India, "the greatest and, to speak the truth, the only social revolution ever heard of in Asia").[27] The liberationists have often gone to school with the oppressors, who commonly claim to represent a more "advanced" culture—materially, intellectually, and militarily. Moses in Egypt is the classic example; he was raised in the palace of the Pharaoh and was certainly more at ease with the Egyptian elite than with the people he came to lead. Sigmund Freud claimed that Moses was actually an Egyptian; whatever he was by birth, he was culturally a man of Egypt.[28]

The training of the liberator in the home country and culture of the oppressor is a common theme in the history of national liberation. Nehru spent eight years in British schools (Harrow; Trinity College, Cambridge; and the Inns of Court) and, as a young man, was probably more conversant with the history and politics of Britain than with the history and politics of India. Late in his life, he told the American ambassador John Kenneth Galbraith, "I am the last Englishman to rule in India."[29] B. R. Ambedkar, the untouchable (Dalit) lawyer and Nehru's first minister of justice, received both a master's degree and a doctorate from Columbia University and the London School of Economics; he also studied for the bar at Gray's Inn. Several leaders of the Indian Communist Party were educated in England and, in an ironic reproduction of the colonial relationship, received their instructions from the Comintern via the Communist Party of Great Britain, whose militants had closer ties to Moscow.[30]

Theodor Herzl, author of *Der Judenstaat*, was another entirely typical nationalist leader. With a very good Austrian education and not much of a Jewish education, he knew far more about other nations than about his own and was at home with the idea of Jewish statehood because he was at home with people who already had a state. Chaim Weizmann, Israel's first president, studied in German universities and then secured a position as research scholar and lecturer in the University of Manchester, where he became a political Anglophile.

Frantz Fanon received his medical and psychiatric education in France and also studied literature and philosophy there. None of the other leaders or intellectuals of the FLN went to school in France, but almost all of them

attended French lycées in Algeria, and many of them
(Fanon too) served in the French and Free French armies—
another kind of education. Ben Bella received France's
highest military honor and a kiss on each cheek from
Charles de Gaulle himself.

Often the leaders of the oppressed identify with an
oppositional ideology in the imperial country—like the
Marxism of some FLNers, or the Fabian socialism of
Nehru and the Indian National Congress (Winston Chur-
chill was simply wrong when he called Nehru a communist), or the east European social democracy of David
Ben-Gurion and Mapai, the dominant party in the Zionist movement and then in Israel's first three decades. But
the oppositional nature of a doctrine in, say, England,
didn't make it familiar in India. Here, too, the militants of
national liberation are the carriers of ideas that are largely
unknown to the people, or most of the people, to whom
they are carrying them.

What can the militants tell the people? They can say
that the people are oppressed because they are backward, passive, mired in superstition and ignorance, "un-
exposed to modern scientific rationality" (to quote Nehru
again), led by men who are the accommodators in chief,
the accomplices of oppression. The militants raise the
hope of newness and give it body in one of the modernist
ideologies—nationalist, liberal, socialist, or some combi-

nation of these three. They promise enlightenment, scientific knowledge, and material advance, but perhaps more
importantly, they promise victory over the oppressors
and equal standing in the world. They appeal especially to
the young (they are usually young themselves) and often
urge a radical break with family and friends and with all
forms of established authority. They demand total commitment to the movement or perhaps a physical move to
an all-encompassing community (like the Zionist kibbutz
or a Gandhian village cooperative). The old ways must be
repudiated and overcome—totally. But the old ways are
cherished by many of the men and women whose ways
they are. That is the paradox of liberation.

II

Still, the liberators do win; they lead a genuinely national
struggle against the foreign rulers of their people. No
doubt, the people themselves are far less sympathetic to
the culture and politics of their rulers than the liberators
are, and once a vanguard of militants has demonstrated
that victory is possible, many men and women who don't
share the ideology of liberation nonetheless join the
struggle. The traditional political and religious leaders
are pushed to the side, or they withdraw (passivity is their
style), or they go along with the liberators, accepting a

marginal role. The odd man out in this schematic story is Mohandas Gandhi, who succeeded in turning traditionalist passivity into a modern political weapon. There is no comparable figure in Zionist history or in or near the FLN—or in any other national liberation movement that I know about. Even when Gandhi openly opposed Hindu beliefs and practices, he spoke to the people in a religious language that was largely foreign to the other leaders of the national liberation movement. In 1934, for example, he suggested that an earthquake in Bihar was divine punishment for the sin of untouchability. Nehru, who would one day help draft a constitution that abolished untouchability, found this remark "staggering." He wrote, "Anything more opposed to the scientific outlook would be difficult to imagine." On occasion, reports B.R. Nanda, the founder and first director of the Nehru Memorial Library, "Gandhi appeared to Jawaharlal as 'a medieval Catholic saint.'"[31] The comment reveals the cultural references that guided Nehru's political judgments (a more local description of Gandhi was certainly possible). The two men managed to work together, but it was crucial to their cooperation that Gandhi conceded the political succession to the secularist and modernist Nehru.

Still, secularists and modernists blame Gandhi for the

surprising strength of religious nationalism in liberated India. Thus V. S. Naipaul:

> The drama that is being played out in India today is the drama that [Gandhi] set up sixty years ago . . . Gandhi gave India its politics; he called up its archaic religious emotions. He made them serve one another, and brought about an awakening. But in independent India the elements of that awakening negate one another. No government can survive on Gandhian fantasy; and . . . spirituality, the solace of a conquered people, which Gandhi turned into a form of national assertion, has soured more obviously into the nihilism that it always was.[32]

That censure was written in the late 1970s; leftist intellectuals in India these days are even more critical of the Gandhian legacy. I will come back to their arguments in the third chapter of this book.

In Israel and Algeria, the transition from national liberation to religious revival was accomplished without the mediating role of a Gandhi figure—so perhaps Gandhi in India was less central than his critics believe; perhaps Hindutva, the ideology of Hindu-ness, would be a powerful presence in Indian politics even if he had never inspired and led the liberation movement. Still, the story is

harder to tell without him or without anyone like him. I
don't mean that other liberationist leaders were unwilling
to speak in religious terms. Zionist writers could hardly
help but invoke the sacred geography of the biblical texts;
their hope for an "ingathering of the exiles" was a secularized version of a messianic promise. In Algeria, the FLN's
first magazine was called *El Moudjahid* (an embarrassment
for Fanon, who told his readers that this term "originally"
meant a Muslim holy warrior but now meant nothing
more than a "fighter"), and the FLN flag was green and
white—green is the traditional color of Islam.[33] What
united Arabs and Berbers in rejecting assimilation, writes
John Dunn in his *Modern Revolutions*, "was the common
tie of Islam under the pressure of colonial occupation."[34]
Indeed, Islam drew a clear line between native Algerians
and European colonizers: "The only thing the colonial
elite was not and, a few ambiguous cases aside, could not
become," writes Geertz, "was Muslim."[35] Algerian militants insisted on their respect for "Islamic principles"—
banning the use of alcohol, for example, within the FLN
and, where they could, among the people generally. Still,
neither the strategy and tactics nor the long-term political agenda of the militants was significantly influenced by
their people's religion. Even the Zionists aimed at a "normal" rather than a redemptive state. Gandhi remains a
very large exception.

So what happened? The traditionalists seemed to be defeated or marginalized; the aura of liberation didn't attach to them; they didn't have much influence in shaping the constitutional arrangements, the economy, or the educational system of the new states; they didn't make much of an appearance among the new political elites. The story is more complicated in Algeria, where political authoritarianism, nascent in the FLN (though opposed by a number of leading militants), triumphed early on. The radical left regime of Ben Bella lasted only three years and was replaced by a more traditional military dictatorship. Houari Boumedienne, who overthrew Ben Bella in 1965, was certainly no Francophile. He had been educated in Muslim schools in Algeria and had studied for a year at El Azhar University in Cairo.[36] But the political leaders he most admired were Castro and Tito; he ran a socialist economy, which had always been the promise of the FLN, and sustained a form of politics that, while socially conservative (on issues like the status of women), would appear to the next generation of Algerian Muslims to have been radically secular. How, then, was political Islam, how were the political versions of Hinduism and Judaism, sustained or invented in the new world of liberation?

The story is different in each of my cases, but there are, again, common features. Some are peripheral to my interests here but perhaps critical to any full causal account.

The militants of the ruling parties, Congress, Mapai, and the FLN, unchallenged in the early years of statehood, grew complacent and tired, and their immediate successors were often opportunists, more interested in power and its rewards than in liberation. Indeed, corruption seems to set in on roughly the same time schedule as religious revival—and the revivalists are not only zealous, they are also righteous (at least until they come to power). But we might expect a tired and complacent Indian National Congress, say, to be confronted by liberationists to its left, like the socialists J. P. Narayan or Asoka Mehta.[37] Early on, it looked as if the Socialist Party would become a leading contender for power in India, but it failed to establish itself in opposition, probably for the same reasons that Congress faltered in government. The decisive challenge to both came from Hindu militants. In Israel and Algeria, too, left oppositionists gave way to religious nationalists and zealots. Why?

In all three countries, religion remained a force in everyday life during the years of liberation and its aftermath. Nationalist leaders often found religion useful for their most immediate political purpose: sustaining the unity of the anticolonial struggle in the new state. Although a few of the militants might have liked to mount a Bolshevik-style attack on religion, the new rulers did not dare do that; perhaps the Russian example was already a warning against a totalizing secularism. In any case, they believed that decline was the destiny of all religions; what Nehru called the "scientific outlook" was bound to triumph. Secularization did not require radical coercion, and it allowed for temporary compromises, because it was an inevitable historical tendency. "Some Hindus dream of going back to the Vedas," Nehru wrote in *The Discovery of India*, "some Muslims dream of an Islamic theocracy. Idle fancies, for there is no going back to the past . . . There is only one-way traffic in Time."[38] The Zionist perspective was strikingly similar, as the historian Ehud Luz writes: "The assumption that the Jewish religion . . . was destined to pass from the scene sooner or later, because it contradicted the needs of modern life, was accepted by practically all the Zionist intelligentsia."[39]

That is more or less what we all believed in those years and for many years after, social scientists and political activists alike. Or, it's what almost all of us believed. Clifford Geertz, who studied nationalist movements in both Indonesia and the Arab world and whose work on Islam I have already cited, thought otherwise. Writing about religion in Bali, in the new Indonesian state in the early 1960s, he argued that religious belief might be swamped by "modern materialist ideas," but probably not. For "such overall drifts—when they do not turn out to be mirages altogether—often pass over deeply rooted cultural configurations with rather less effect upon them than we would have thought possible." He went further, suggesting that "today in Bali some of the same social and intellectual processes that gave rise to the fundamental religious transformations of world history seem to be at least well begun."[40] In other places, too, the drift, or perhaps the storm, of national liberation passed over ancient societies and reborn nations with "rather less effect" than the movements' militants expected, and the processes that eventually led to religious revival were already begun, under the eyes of the militants but out of their sight.

The old ways were sustained in temples, synagogues, and mosques, but also, and perhaps more importantly, in interpersonal relations, in families and in life-cycle celebrations, where the sustaining behaviors were hardly visible to secular militants busily at work on the big projects of modernization. Indeed, the coming revivals were fueled by the resentment that ordinary people, pursuing their customary ways, felt toward those secularizing and modernizing elites, with their foreign ideas, their patronizing attitudes, and their big projects. They were fueled even more by the authoritarian or paternalist politics that was forced upon the new elites in their war against the customary ways. Some would argue that authoritarianism was not so much forced upon as embraced by the elites: the idea of modernity, writes Ashis Nandy, a critic of Nehruvian secularism, gave its protagonists "seemingly deservedly, a disproportionate access to state power."[41]

The authoritarianism of Boumedienne's Algerian state was particularly brutal; indeed, the politics of the FLN before liberation was already murderous, reaching to a full-scale civil war between the FLN and Mesali Hadj's National Algerian Movement (where many of the leaders of the FLN had gotten their political training)—some ten thousand Algerians were killed.[42] By contrast, the Indian National Congress and the Labor Zionists were committed to democracy and mostly managed their internal tensions in nonviolent ways. But even the leaders of these movements, when they exercised political power, did so with a sure sense that they knew what was best for their backward and often recalcitrant peoples.

Then the backwardness came back—and the democracy that the liberationists created (even in Algeria, briefly, from 1989 to 1991) was the chief instrument of its return. "The present crisis of liberal democracy [in India]," writes the political theorist Rajeev Bhargava, "is due in large part to its own success." Religious men and women, previously passive and inarticulate, entered the newly created public domain in numbers that "greatly exceeded" the number in the "tiny upper crust that led the national movement." Democratic politics encouraged "ethno-religious political mobilization," and the mobilized men and women did not "come from a cultural background with an obviously liberal or democratic character."[43]

But it wasn't the old backwardness that these people, or the politicians they followed, brought back. Religion appeared now, as I've already suggested, in militant, ideological, and politicized forms—modern even in its anti-modernism. Its protagonists claim to embody the ancient traditions, the faith of the ancestors, even to represent a pure, authentic version of it; oldness is their mantra. And although the claim is false, the sense of oldness must account, at least in part, for the appeal of their program. They connect the liberated people to their own past; they provide a sense of belonging and stability in a rapidly changing world. With the old imperial oppressors gone, they also provide recognizable, even familiar "others" as objects of fear or hate—who can be blamed for all that has gone wrong since the day of liberation. Sometimes the "others" are members of a rival religion; sometimes they are "Westernizing" leftists, secularists, heretics, and infidels—traitors, it is said, in our midst.

But what happened to the Indian, the Israeli, and the Algerian newness? Where are the new men and women, each the equal of the others, standing straight, tall, and smart? I am not sure how to answer that question. There are a lot of people like that—national liberation reached beyond the tiny upper crust—but nowhere near as many as the liberationists expected. The culture of liberation was apparently too thin to sustain these people and enable them to reproduce themselves; the radical rejection of the past left, as it were, too little material for cultural construction. The liberators did generate a set of holidays, a set of heroes, a set of commemorative rituals; they made up songs and dances; they wrote novels and poems (compare the French Revolution with its new calendar, its neoclassical revival, its fetes and pageantry). For a while, enough people seemed to engage with all these so that it was almost possible to believe in the new beginning. But the newness was too artificial, too recently constructed, and after a couple of generations, the heroes lost their aura, the commemorations lost their charm; young people drifted away, moving toward the excitements of global pop culture or toward the fervency of religious revival. The attraction of pop culture is no doubt a disappointment to the aging militants of national liberation, but their biggest disappointment, their biggest surprise, is the large number of young men and women who are drawn to the ideologies of Hindutva, messianic Zionism and ultra-Orthodox Judaism, and radical Islam. And aren't they right to be surprised? Daughters of the women whose self-uprooting Fanon celebrated are willingly rerooting themselves, returning to religious faiths that are—at least to this secular eye—as misogynist as ever. Isn't this unbelievable?

I suppose it is believable after all; it is just the sort of thing that social science claims to be able to explain or at least to understand. Marxist writers, who are committed to scientific explanation, search for the social class whose material interests religious revivalism might serve. A recent study of "left discourses in contemporary India" finds different writers attributing the rise of Hindutva to the petty bourgeoisie (the classic Marxist candidate) and also to the rich peasants, the poor peasants, the lumpen proletariat, the urban workers, the old Brahmins, and the new capitalists. I have some sympathy with a despairing comment that appeared in the leftist magazine *Economic and Political Weekly* in 1993: "Whatever the analytical difficulties of reducing an ideology to its material base, unless one posits . . . such an epistemological relation, one will be left with a politically debilitating agnosticism." But either the reduction doesn't work or it needs more work. Two years later, the same writer in the same magazine wrote that Hindutva isn't only "an instrumentality protecting a material interest . . . Over and above that, it is a set of values, attitudes, and norms of behavior that can only be countered with the aid of alternative values and norms."[44]

That acknowledgment seems to me the beginning of understanding. I wouldn't give up on the search for a material base. Marxist writers are right to look for the people most likely to benefit from what V. P. Varma identifies as the central goal of Hindu revivalism, "the restoration of the Vedic principles [that require] the functional organization of society."[45] The old elites, the upper castes, new capitalists, and patriarchs everywhere, in the family, the local community, and the state—these are the obvious beneficiaries. Still, it is necessary to acknowledge the populist appeal of revivalism, the staying power of the old religion up and down the social hierarchy. Without that appeal the religious revival would be of no use to Brahmins, capitalists, and patriarchs. Countering the revival with a set of alternative values and norms is not so easy; doing it ex nihilo seems pretty much impossible.

But perhaps the militants of national liberation, like all revolutionaries, had to insist on radical cultural negation—in Ambedkar's words, the "complete destruction of Brahminism . . . as a social order"—and then on radical newness.[46] Perhaps that is the essential or necessary character of their project. Years ago, when I was writing about the Puritan revolution in England, I came upon a sermon preached in the House of Commons in 1643 that expresses a sentiment common to revolutionaries everywhere: "Take heed of building upon an old frame," the preacher told the MPs, "that must be all plucked down to the ground. Take heed of plastering when you should be pulling down."[47] The difficulty is that such a radical pulling down doesn't appeal to the people living in the house; they are too attached to it, even if they recognize, even if they complain about, its discomforts. Maybe what is necessary is only a partial demolition and a renovation of the rest—a renovation, that is, of values and norms.

There actually were intellectuals in the national liberation movements who aimed at a critical engagement with the old culture rather than a total attack upon it. I like to think that had they won, the story might have turned out differently. The liberators might have made their peace with at least some part of their nation's past, fashioned a set of beliefs and practices that were new but also familiar, and avoided the extremism of religious revival. Maybe. I want to argue something like that, but it's best to begin with skepticism. Some commentators insist that engagement was never possible and place their hopes in the dialectic: first comes the politics of radical secularist rejection, then the politics of militant religious reaffirmation, and then, as the *Oxford English Dictionary* says, "the contradictions merge . . . in a higher truth that comprehends them both." But the dialectic doesn't seem to be working these days the way it used to. I don't see many signs of the coming synthesis. In India, Israel, and Algeria—and probably in other places—the struggle that the liberationists thought they had won still has to be won. Secular liberation hasn't been defeated, but it has been challenged in unexpected ways and with unexpected strength. The struggle is going to continue for a long time, and its outcome is as uncertain as it was at the very beginning. Like the ancient Israelites, the modern militants thought they had reached the promised land, only to discover that they carried Egypt in their baggage.

TWO

The Paradox Illustrated

Zionism vs. Judaism

I

Zionism is one of the success stories of twentieth-century national liberation. The first generation of Zionist leaders proposed a solution to the "Jewish question" that to just about every realistic Jew and non-Jew in the world seemed impossible to realize, and the next generation realized it. The realization came too late for most of the Jews of Europe; it is darkened by the greatest catastrophe in Jewish history. Nonetheless, Zionism reached the unreachable goal that Theodor Herzl set for it, within the fifty-year time span that he envisioned.

Viewed in historical perspective, Israel is a much greater surprise than India or Algeria, whose nations were liberated, as it were, in place. The Zionist movement, born in exile, managed to establish a sovereign state in what Herzl called an "old-new land," inhabited mostly by Arabs and colonized by the Ottoman Turks and the British. Today, Jewish self-determination, impossible for almost two thousand years, is an everyday fact. So why isn't that the end of the story? Everything after independence is "post-Zionist." What we should talk about now is Palestinian national liberation.

But the Zionist victory is more complicated than this brief telling suggests, and it is complicated in much the same way as the victories of the Indian National Congress and the Algerian FLN. Zionism isn't entirely a success; its liberationist project isn't yet completed. What I called in the first chapter the paradox of national liberation has its specifically Jewish version, which is my subject here.

Imagine that a group of the Zionist "founders" found themselves in contemporary Israel, a ghostly congress discussing the history of the movement. A few of the *Bilu'im*, the earliest settlers, would be there; some cultural Zionists, followers of Ahad Ha'am, would join the discussion; representatives of the Herzlian or political Zionists would certainly be there, and also a delegation from Chaim Weizmann's Democratic Faction; the early socialists, Labor Zionists from the Second Aliyah, the future hegemonic group, would be a large presence; and a few of the Miz-

rahi rabbis, the Orthodox minority who supported the
Zionist project, would attend.[1] Most of these people, I believe, would not think that their hopes had been fully realized. The state as it is today would not match their vision;
even the political Zionists, who were often said to want
nothing but a state, any state, anywhere, had a particular
state in mind—and Israel isn't quite that kind of state. It
also isn't the kind of state that the Mizrahi rabbis had in
mind, but I shall focus on the expectations and disappoint-
ments of the others, for Zionism was, at its center and in
the years of its greatest achievements, overwhelmingly a
secular project. That's what makes its relation to Judaism
so interesting. I propose to look closely at that relationship, taking it as a special case of the internal tension or
contradiction illustrated also in the history of national
liberation in India and Algeria—and in Palestine. This
further case is bound to come up, for Palestine already,
even before statehood, has its own history of secular nationalism and religious revival.

II

The Jewish version of the story begins with exile. Over
the course of almost two thousand years, a span of time
that our imaginations cannot easily encompass, the stateless and scattered people of Israel developed a religious/

political culture adapted to statelessness and scattered-
ness. I don't know how long it takes to develop a culture of
that kind. We can find signs of the adaptation very early
on—as in Jeremiah's famous letter to the exiles in Babylonia
sometime around 587 BCE (the prophet speaks, as always,
in God's name): "Build houses and live in them, plant gar-
dens and eat their fruit . . . And seek the welfare of the city
to which I have exiled you and pray to the Lord in its behalf; for in its prosperity you shall prosper."[2] But the social
construction of exile as the prototypical Jewish condition
took many centuries, and the construction is very powerful. It is the deep architecture of Jewish life. Judaism in
the late nineteenth century, when Zionism was born, was
a religion of exile. A yearning for return to the long-lost
homeland played an important part in that religion; the
idea of political independence played no part at all. The
Jewish people had forgotten, wrote Leo Pinsker in *Auto-
Emancipation*, what political independence is.[3]

Exilic politics had only two aspects. First, Jews submit-
ted to gentile rule; they practiced a politics of deference.
Second, they patiently waited for divine redemption; they
practiced a politics of deferred hope. In fact, a lot more
can be said about the political experience of the Jews, but
it is this dualism that is reflected in their law and literature. Jewish submission would last until the coming of
the Messiah, and the coming of the Messiah was in God's

hands and seemed to be indefinitely postponed.[4] Deference and deferment: the words and practices that this politics (or anti-politics) required had to be reinvented in each Diaspora setting. But the inventions were in no sense makeshift; nor would it be right to say that the politics of exile was reluctantly accepted. This was the natural politics of the Jews in the eyes of the Jews themselves, the necessary consequence, so it was commonly thought, of the place that God had assigned them in world history.

It follows, then, that any political effort to escape from the exile, any nationalism aiming at statehood and sovereignty, would have to be the work of people who rejected this divine assignment, who broke with the culture of deference and deferment. But since this culture was a central part of Judaism as it existed in the nineteenth century, Zionism was, and could only be, the creation of people who were hostile to Judaism. If pressed, I would qualify that statement in all sorts of ways, but in its naked form, unqualified, it helps to explain a centrally important Zionist goal: "negation of the exile." This is not the same as the end of the exile. Of course, Zionists wanted to bring the exile to an end, but they also believed, or many of them believed, that ending it would be impossible without first "negating" the cultural predispositions and habits, the mentality, of the exile. "Everything," Albert Memmi wrote, "is paralyzed, fettered, and inhibited" by that mentality.[5] To escape exile it was necessary for the Jews to overcome their long-term adaptation to captivity among the gentiles. The name of that adaptation was "Judaism."

Overcoming the mentality of exile was a project that could find support within the Jewish world, but its most prominent and successful advocates were likely to be Jews who had assimilated into the world of their oppressors and who viewed their own people with a foreign eye. Herzl, a nationalist leader of exactly that kind, wanted the Jews to have a state like any European state. This Zionist dream of normality, which looks back to the demand of the biblical elders in First Samuel 8—"We will have a king over us, that we also may be like all the nations"—is born out of persecution and fear, but it also has two intellectual sources, both of them at odds with exilic culture. The first is a close-up knowledge of other nations, and the second is a belief that imitation of these other nations is both possible and desirable. Indeed, Herzl imitated the most progressive European ideas, especially with regard to the status of women. In his Zionist utopia, *Old-New Land* (1902), women have "equal rights" with men and are obligated, like men, to do two years of national service.[6] Herzl doesn't explicitly set this equality against traditional Judaism's exclusion of women from all public roles, but it is an obvious challenge to the tradition.

Leaders like Herzl and Max Nordau, his most prominent intellectual supporter, had no second thoughts, no anxieties, about the negation of the exile, because nothing in their experience suggested that what was being negated contained much of value; they had few sentimental ties to the old way of life—what Herzl called the "thousand-year-old hereditary disease."[7] This may be the key to their effectiveness; they are single-minded in pursuit of their goals.

But this same alienation from the people they mean to liberate can bring down the leaders of national liberation movements—as the Uganda episode suggests in Herzl's case. The story is probably sufficiently well known that I can discuss it briefly.[8] It began in 1903, when a British colonial official suggested that a large tract of territory in Uganda might be made available for Jewish settlement—in lieu of Palestine. Herzl was eager to accept the offer, which represented the first official recognition of the Zionist movement as a territorial claimant; he apparently had little sense of the opposition it would arouse. Zionist leaders closer to their people understood immediately, instinctively, that this was negation gone one step too far. However desperate the condition of the Jews (the Uganda debate unfolded immediately after the Kishinev pogrom in Russia), a specifically Jewish nationalism could have only one country as its object, Eretz Yisrael, the Land of Israel. These leaders, most of them Russian Jews, wanted to acknowledge the British offer with gratitude and then reject it (which is what happened three or four years later, after Herzl's death).

In a curious way, the idea of settling Jews in Uganda, under British rule, was simultaneously too radical and too conservative. Its radicalism appealed to (some) secularist and socialist Zionists, who worried that the mystique of the Land of Israel would make the work of cultural transformation more difficult—or perhaps defeat it entirely. Years earlier, a prominent advocate of Jewish enlightenment, Judah Leib Levin, had argued against settlement in Palestine (he preferred America): "I worried about the orthodox and feared the rabbis, because of the air of *Eretz Yisrael*, permeated with ancient prejudices, [where] the *maskilim* [the enlightened intellectuals] would be unable to bring their influence to bear."[9] Hillel Zeitlin put the argument even more forcefully during the Uganda controversy—and in a way that resonates today: "The same tradition that burdens us in the Diaspora will burden us a thousand times more in *Eretz Yisrael*, because that is its home. The rabbinic dominion over the masses will not be weakened there, as the freethinking Zionists hope, but on the contrary will get stronger and stronger."[10] Uganda (or at least the idea of Uganda) offered a new beginning, a chance to establish national life on a modern footing.

At the same time, however, a Ugandan settlement would also be a continuation of the exile and the subjection it entailed. The new rulers would certainly be more benign than the old; the king of England was far preferable to the Russian tsar or the Turkish sultan, but he was not King David; he did not represent Jewish sovereignty. That may be why the Mizrahi rabbis were so comfortable with Herzl's scheme: they would not have to face the challenge of sovereignty.[11] At one of the earliest Zionist meetings, the Kattowitz conference in 1884, an Orthodox delegate from Romania argued against political independence for reasons that may seem trivial to contemporary secular Jews (and non-Jews) but in fact go to the heart of the conflict between Zionism and Judaism: No state, he said, can maintain itself without a postal service, railways, and the telegraph, and these have to be operated day and night throughout the week. "But if the officials of Israel were to rest on the Sabbath, according to the laws of Moses, other states . . . would protest, while if we were to permit our officials to violate the Sabbath and the festivals, our brethren . . . would rise up and destroy us."[12] Other examples abound: the maintenance of gas (and, soon, electricity) services, police work and firefighting (if lives were at stake, these would be permitted; if not, not), the ordinary functioning of hospitals and clinics, garbage collection, street cleaning, and so on. In the lands of the exile, gentiles did all this necessary work on the Sabbath; in Uganda the British presumably would arrange for it to be done.

Religious Jews could not yet imagine doing it themselves. In their private lives, they relied on the "Shabbos goy," a gentile friend, neighbor, or servant, to perform all the necessary chores forbidden to Jews on the Sabbath—and what was the state, what else could it be in pre-messianic times, but a large-scale Shabbos goy?

I doubt that Herzl ever worried about the possible incompatibility of the laws of Moses and a Jewish state; his visionary description of a state where the army would stay in its barracks and the rabbis in their synagogues did not include the laws.[13] From a political standpoint, the sacred geography of the Jews should have worried him more, but he had little sense of that either until the Uganda controversy erupted. Accounts of his conversations with British officials suggest that he argued for as much autonomy as he could get in a Ugandan setting; the setting itself was of less importance to him. And yet sacred geography was one feature of exilic culture that neither he nor any of the other Ugandans (later they called themselves "Territorialists") could negate.

The cultural Zionists, followers of Ahad Ha'am ("One of the People"—the pen name of Asher Ginzberg), opposed the Uganda plan and sharply criticized Herzl's lack of Jewish culture and learning—and, even more, his insensitivity to Jewish emotional attachments. They regularly insisted on the need for continuity with the past, and a few of them, like the poet Hayim Nahman Bialik, aimed consciously at a critical engagement with, rather than a negation of, the exile. Bialik's call for a cultural "ingathering," alongside or even before the demographic ingathering, suggests the road not taken, which I will defend later on as the better path.[14] Ahad Ha'am himself attacked Zionist writers who understood the whole of Jewish history "to be one long mistake that requires immediate, complete rectification." Although he acknowledged in a private letter that Zionism may involve a "latent contradiction [with Judaism] deep within the soul," he consistently opposed what he called "defiant apostasy [*apikorsut le-hakhis*—the phrase is taken from the Talmud]."[15] Nonetheless, his own ideas about continuity were selective, focused mainly on "prophetic morality," and the ideas of many of his followers and admirers were more selective still.

Zionism is in no sense a "direct continuation of the ancient culture," wrote Leo Motzkin. "Even though it means to refashion something rather than create something *ex nihilo*," argued Joseph Klausner, "Zionism is a highly radical Jewish movement . . . It aspires to a total revolution in Jewish life: to a revolt against the diaspora." A total revolution: there was little in Jewish life and culture that would be spared by these Jewish liberators. Isaiah Berlin's essay on Chaim Weizmann beautifully illustrates this paradoxical point. Weizmann was at one with his people, Berlin says: "his language was theirs, and their view of life was his." Yet he recognized the people as "a semihelot population, relegated to an inferior and dependent status, which produced in them the virtues and vices of slaves." For this condition, Weizmann thought "there was no remedy save a revolution—a total social transformation." Men like Motzkin, Klausner, and Weizmann would probably have agreed with Simon Bernfeld that "it is impossible to ensure the future of a nation by destroying its past"; still, there was much that they wanted to destroy.[16]

The chief object of their critique was religion itself—a point made most strongly by Haim Hazaz in a short story, "The Sermon," written in the 1940s: "Zionism and Judaism are not at all the same, but two things quite different from each other, and maybe even two things directly opposite to each other . . . When a man can no longer be a Jew, he becomes a Zionist."[17] In partial disagreement with this radical position, Martin Buber insisted that he was opposed only to Judaism's decadent, exilic forms—to "the subjugated spirituality and the [imposed] tradition . . . drained of its meaning."[18] Like him, many of the cultural Zionists, and later the socialists, looked to biblical Israel for inspiration: to a culture of kings, warriors, and prophets that they could hope to continue. But the biblical heroes described in Zionist literature and propaganda seemed to be the exact opposites of contemporary Jews; and their creed was very far from contemporary Judaism. It nourished strong men and women, whereas the religion of exile, in Zionist eyes, produced political passivity and resignation, a slave mentality that was incapable of resistance or self-help. To turn to the Bible was to acknowledge a break, a cultural chasm.

As if in illustration of the Zionist thesis, Israel Kagan, a leading Orthodox rabbi, insisted that "it is not in our power to repair the condition of our people, because we are under the domination of our enemies."[19] Statements like that were taken by Zionist writers to represent the "lack of national self-respect and self-confidence, of political initiative and unity," produced by years of exile and religious resignation.[20] But Kagan would have said that domination was God's decree, and that political strength was not the only source of self-respect. The gap between these views was very wide, and it wasn't easy to find continuities.

Sometimes the Zionist critique was less doctrinal, more immediate—as when writers, mostly very young, attacked the turning away from physical activity and the natural world that characterized exilic life. "Secular Zionism," as David Hartman says, was marked by "a passionate yearning for new anthropological models that celebrated the dignity of . . . physical power."[21] It was also marked by a passionate hatred of the "physical degeneracy" of east European Jewry. Indeed, the anti-Semitic stereotype of the pale, stooped, fearful Jew is also a Zionist stereotype. In an ardent eulogy for Herzl, written in 1906, the young Ze'ev Jabotinsky provides a strong example. He asks, How should we portray the future Hebrew?—and responds:

> Our starting point is to take the typical Yid of today and to imagine his diametrical opposite . . . Because the Yid is ugly, sickly, and lacks decorum, we shall endow the ideal image of the Hebrew with masculine beauty. The Yid is trodden upon and easily frightened and, therefore, the Hebrew ought to be proud and independent . . . The Yid has accepted submission and, therefore, the Hebrew ought to learn to command. The Yid wants to conceal his identity from strangers and, therefore, the Hebrew should look the world straight in the eye and declare: "I am a Hebrew!"[22]

The emphasis here on beauty, pride, and power points to Jabotinsky's future as a Zionist of the right. Ahad Ha'am, by contrast, was more concerned with the specifically intellectual qualities bred by centuries of subjection: "the lack of unity and order . . . the lack of [common] sense and social cohesion . . . the narcissism that holds such terrible sway over the prominent members of the people . . . the thrill of showing off and the arrogance . . .

the tendency always to be too clever." This kind of diatribe has many counterparts in other nationalist and revolutionary movements. I cannot resist a comparison, possibly unfair to Ahad Ha'am, with Lenin's critique of Russian intellectuals: he charges them with "slovenliness . . . carelessness, untidiness, unpunctuality, nervous haste, the inclination to substitute discussion for action, talk for work, the inclination to undertake everything under the sun without finishing anything."[23] The list of complaints is different, but the tone is very much the same, and I don't think that these two men, for all their differences, would have had much difficulty agreeing on what they disliked in their contemporaries.

So Zionism was marked simultaneously by a deep commitment to the Jewish people and by an equally deep commitment to the transformation of the Jews. "These youngsters," wrote Aharon Eisenberg, a moderate religious nationalist, "are frantically opposed to our traditions, which have been sanctified by the people, yet they claim that everything they are doing is intended to save the people . . . And some even say that the people cannot be saved unless they [the youngsters] first destroy everything the people [have] built with their blood."[24] Destroyed and saved: let me illustrate the transformation these militants hoped for with a list of contrasting cultural values and attitudes. The columns are here labeled

"from" and "to," and the paired terms form a coherent
and more or less self-explanatory whole.

passivity	activity
fearfulness	courage
deference	pride
obedience	rebellion
weakness	strength
indoors	outdoors
peddlers/shopkeepers	farmers/workers
subordination of women	gender equality
dependence	independence
subjection	citizenship
isolation from the world	engagement with the world
fear and hatred of gentiles	equality and friendship with gentiles

Many Jewish intellectuals and professionals in the
West believed that the transformation represented by the
second term in each pair required only emancipation,
civic equality in the lands of the exile. Jews would become
British or French or German citizens and then lead "normal" lives. They would be liberated in place; they would
leave the ghetto but not the Diaspora. And then they
would be active, proud, strong, and engaged with the world
around them—and if they weren't, the reasons would be

individual reasons, as with their gentile neighbors. The cultural Zionists thought this belief an illusion, but they also, and more importantly, thought it was an exilic illusion, another sign of the loss of self-respect. Emancipation was simply the latest version of subjection, a new way to defer to the gentiles. Typically, it did not require a critique of religious belief: it was perfectly compatible with the faith of Moses as defined by the rabbis. But it did require the surrender of any claim to national self-determination. Ahad Ha'am's essay "Slavery in Freedom" (1891) is a bitter critique of Western Jewry, who, in his view, had sold their heritage for meager and purely private advantage.[25] At the same time, the closed, narrow, vulnerable, and frightened world of Orthodoxy in the East—where the heritage took its most visible form—was no better; it represented slavery within slavery. Zionism aimed at an escape from both; this required collective action, cultural and political. But assimilated Jews no longer acknowledged the collectivity, and religious Jews would wait forever for God to act. Both forms of exilic consciousness had to be negated.

Zionist success was the work of "new Jews" who embodied this negation. There can't be any doubt about the newness, although plenty of old Jews appeared in and around the Zionist movement, and the line between new and old was nowhere as clear as I am pretending. Nor were all the new Jews heroic pioneers, working the land, as in Zionist legend. Nor were there all that many of them. Zionism was not a mass movement; it always had a certain elitist character, a preference for quality over quantity, since, after all, the negation of an ancient culture is not a popular cause. The vanguard of new Jews included political activists and even politicians of a kind normal in modern secular societies but rare in the old Jewish communities; also soldiers, bureaucrats, managers, professionals, intellectuals—and farmers and workers. What made them new was that they did not accept rabbinic authority, they were not deferential to their gentile (Turkish and British) rulers, and they refused to defer their hope for national independence.

Ahad Ha'am had a precise picture of how these people would bring about change. First they would transform themselves; next they would create a "spiritual center" in Palestine and, working outward from the center, slowly transform the general culture of exilic Jewry; then, slowly again, they would create a political center and ultimately (perhaps) an independent state.[26] But this gradualist prospect was shattered by the urgencies of twentieth-century Jewish life. In the event, the vanguard created the state and won the wars that statehood required long before the cultural transformation was completed.

Once the state was established, its first task was the ingathering of the exiles—first, the surviving Jews of central and eastern Europe, displaced persons desperate for a place, then the Jews of North Africa and Mesopotamia, living under threat because of the eclipse of empire and the rise of local nationalisms. The ingathering was a huge success; hundreds of thousands of immigrants poured into the new state. Its most dramatic effect, however, was to bring home the un-negated culture of the exile. So what Zionism in the Diaspora had not accomplished, the new Zionist state set out to accomplish. The absorption of immigrants was designed as a process of cultural transformation; it represented the continuation of the earlier cultural war by other means. Ben-Gurion's description of what needed to be done, written before the establishment of the state, is instructive:

> [Absorption] means taking . . . uprooted, impoverished, sterile Jewish masses, living parasitically off of an alien economic body and dependent on others— and introducing them to productive and creative life, implanting them on the land, integrating them into primary production in agriculture, in industry and handicraft, and making them economically independent and self-sufficient.[27]

Immigrant absorption was a form of state action, the work of civil servants, teachers, social workers, army instructors.

As Ben-Gurion's verbs suggest, the process was less persuasive than coercive; it was marked by a kind of authoritarianism. As became clear only later on, it was also bitterly resented—and successfully resisted, privately— by many of the immigrants. The cultural transformation intended by Ben-Gurion is now publicly challenged by a revived and militant Judaism.

III

Although important qualifications are necessary, I can tell a similar story about Palestinian national liberation. As I write, the liberationist militants have not won their battle; they are the protagonists of a failed, but not definitively failed, political movement. One day, I hope, there will be a Palestinian state, but the encounter of secular nationalism with a religious revival is already well begun. And the secularists' surprise at the strength of the religious forces is not much different from the surprise expressed in my other cases. The inability to found a Palestinian state no doubt fuels the religious revival, but it doesn't explain it. Had the secularists succeeded, they would still have been challenged by an Islamic fierceness that they did not foresee.[28]

The Palestinian liberationists never went to school with their imperial opponents. They did not study in England,

and they never attended Israeli universities. But many of the earliest leaders of the Palestinian movement, because they were Christians and then because they were Marxists, did look at their own people from a significant critical distance. Militants like George Habash and Waddie Haddad, founders of the Popular Front for the Liberation of Palestine, studied at the American University in Beirut, called themselves Marxist-Leninists, and brutally criticized traditional Arab politics. It would be hard to overestimate the importance of Christian Palestinians like these two in the liberation movement—especially in its most radical and most radically secularist wing.

Yasser Arafat is harder to figure out than the Marxist militants of the Popular Front, but in many ways he fits the picture of the nationalist leader that I sketched in the first chapter. Born in Egypt to parents who left Palestine in 1927, well before the Naqba—the "catastrophe"—of 1948, he came to lead a people whose formative experience he did not share. As one of his biographers writes, "He had no childhood home in the lost homeland, no plot of land which became the possession of someone else, no close relatives who were transformed into destitute refugees."[29] For many years, he worked as an engineer in Kuwait, and it was there that he founded Fatah. The name is an acronym, but the word means "conquering" or "victory" and is often used to describe the early years of Islamic expansion. Arafat, according to all his biographers, was a believing Muslim and by no means a Marxist-Leninist. The organization he founded, however, was secular and nationalist, inspired more by the Algerian FLN and the writings of Frantz Fanon than by the Qur'an.[30] To true believers, Arafat was a typical secularist, committed to the establishment of a national and not an Islamic state. His successors are no different—enemies of God, therefore, who must be replaced.

IV

Let me return for a moment to the general version of the story. Many successful national liberation movements produce, without intending to, an underground culture, a secret traditionalism nourished by memory, carried by the family, sustained in conventicles and in life-cycle ceremonies. The protagonists of this culture pose, Marrano-like, as citizens of the new state: they attend its schools, serve (some of them) in its army, vote in its elections, accept the benefits it provides—without ever allowing themselves to be refashioned in its image. They don't become the new men and women that Ben-Gurion and Fanon celebrated; they don't become modern, secular, liberal, democratic citizens. Rather, their first allegiance is not to the nation-state but to something more like the traditional, pre-state community. After a time, when national liberation has receded in memory, these traditionalists stage a counterrevolution: thus the rise of Islamic radicalism in Algeria (and in Palestine), of Hindutva in India, and of Jewish zealotry in Israel. The religious resurgence is a shock to the national liberation elites, who had grown complacent about the victory of newness.

The traditionalists, however, are not really as close in spirit or creed to their ancestors as they like to think; they may not be liberated, but they are changed by the experience of liberation, often in ways they themselves don't understand. The outcome of the counterrevolution is uncertain. It lies beyond my reach here, for the Indian, Israeli, and Algerian stories are still unfinished. The return of the negated has brought with it a militant religious nationalism that has radically altered the politics of all three countries (and of Palestine, too) but hasn't yet overwhelmed or defeated the liberationist project.

The return of the negated is a general phenomenon, but it is also peculiar to each case, and I want to focus again on Israel. When exilic Jewry comes "home," it brings with it a characteristic politics; this may be concealed for a time behind a facade of conventional citizen-like behavior, but it is possible nonetheless to describe its basic features. (I am not discussing here the arrival of the Soviet Jews, who were modernized and secularized by communism, not by Zionism, and who don't fit neatly into my schematic account.) The politics of religious Jews in Israel follows from the experience of exile and is more closely continuous with it than Zionism is. Israel's ultra-Orthodox Jews, the *Haredim*, the most rapidly growing sector of the population, do not really think of the state as their own. Some of them are fierce nationalists (and very close to the dictionary definition that I quoted in the first chapter), but they don't have the sense that citizens are supposed to have of being responsible for the whole; they don't recognize a "good" that is common to themselves and all other Israelis. They retain a view of the state typical of a stateless people, who are always outsiders, always vulnerable; they are political opportunists, seeking to seize whatever benefits the state provides and escape its burdens. The fellowship of democratic citizens and the freewheeling debates of democratic politics are largely alien to them; they participate in an older fellowship, accept as authoritative the rulings of their rabbis, and vote as a bloc.

Zionism for them, as Amnon Rubinstein has written, is not a "return to the family of nations but its diametric opposite—a new polarization between the Jews and the Gentiles of the earth." The Arab-Israeli conflict gives this polarization a special force, but the view is general: all the "others" are hostile and threatening. "The whole world is on one side and we are on the other," wrote an Orthodox rabbi in the 1970s in an astonishing misrepresentation of the condition of his country, which nonetheless makes Rubinstein's point.[31] "Otherness," on this view, is always close and always dangerous; it includes the world of secular Jewish enlightenment as well as the world of the gentiles.

The return of the negated, one could say, is simply the fulfillment of Hillel Zeitlin's prediction that in the Land of Israel, rabbinic dominion "will not be weakened, as the freethinking Zionists hope, but . . . will get stronger and stronger." Nonetheless, the freethinking Zionists were surprised by the resurgence (and the demographic flourishing) of Orthodox and ultra-Orthodox Judaism. This was true even of Ben-Gurion, who had always worried about the legacy of exilic statelessness: "A people used to Exile, oppressed, lacking independence, for thousands of years, does not change overnight, by fiat . . . into a sovereign, state-bearing people, lovingly and willingly carrying the duties and burdens of independence."[32] Still, Ben-Gurion (like Nehru) was a secular optimist, and when he made his famous deal with the *Haredim* and agreed to the exemption of yeshiva students from the draft, he was sure that the exempted students would be few in number. In the new Jewish state, the *Haredim* would be like the Mennonites and Amish in the United States. He could safely compromise with the rabbis because the future belonged to him and to his fellow freethinking citizens.

Ben-Gurion was wrong (at least his time horizon was wrong), but that mistake is only part of the story. For the revival of traditional Orthodoxy represents only one side of exilic political consciousness, the side of deference, fear, and resentment. The other side is represented by the figure of the Messiah, whose coming was, in the long years of exile, indefinitely deferred. The insistence on waiting for the Messiah and the rabbinic ban on "forcing the end" support the political culture of passivity. On the other hand, the abiding certainty that he will one day come; the intermittent, unforeseen, inexplicable intensifications of expectancy; the appearance of false prophets and messianic pretenders—all these suggest a deep dissatisfaction with that culture. Messianism is simultaneously a comforting fantasy and a disruptive force. Secular Zionists exploited this force, even claimed sometimes to embody it, but in fact they naturalized and tamed it. They made messianism into hard work and redemption into a gradual process of acquisition and renewal: "Another dunam [about a quarter acre of land], another goat." But once the mundane work was done and religious Jews beheld the state, especially the state as it was in the ominously magical moment of 1967, triumphant over its enemies, many of them decided that they did indeed live in messianic times—or, better, on the very brink of messianic times.[33]

National liberation had brought them this far but could take them no further. Now the Messiah waited only for the zeal of the faithful to express itself in political life. Like the Zionist pioneers, the faithful would settle the land, but they would act in fulfillment of divine command, not of a secular ideology, and they would live in accordance with divine law. And then the glorious days would begin.

This vision looks something like, but isn't the same as, romantic blood-and-soil nationalism; nor is it an exaltation of the Israeli state. For the settler militants, the nation-state as it exists today is simply an instrument for promoting God's politics—but not a very reliable instrument. They look forward to a time, as the editor of the settler magazine *Nekudah* argued more than a decade ago, when democracy (an alien Western form of government) will be replaced by an authentically Jewish religious regime that will lead Jews back to a life based on the Torah.[34] Meanwhile, however, messianic enthusiasm doesn't seem constrained by Jewish morality; the settler movement is the most visible and frightening version of the counterrevolution. It isn't entirely responsible for the length of the post-1967 occupation of the West Bank and Gaza or the attendant cruelties, but it has a large part in both.

Contemporary messianism has two faces: it reiterates the old exilic understanding that redemption is the only alternative to exile, but it also supports a radically new and fierce politics; its protagonists do not seek exemption from the draft (and they decry the yeshiva students who do). To advance their version of God's politics, they are more than ready to use military force, which exilic Jews had always identified with the "other"—as many ultra-Orthodox Jews still do. A kind of thuggishness exists on the margins of the settler movement, tolerated and even encouraged by some of its central figures—and nothing more clearly distinguishes the Judaism of the revival from the Judaism of the exile.

But in modern Israel as in exilic history, messianism is likely to have a short life; it is infinitely susceptible to disappointment, disillusion, and new postponements; and post-1967 Jewish messianism, despite the ardor of its militants, has already faded. The real challenge to Zionist liberation comes from a strange (and only partially consummated) merger of messianic militancy with the coming out and rising assertiveness of ultra-Orthodox Jews. Settler Zionism and ultra-Orthodoxy are theologically dissimilar, but their appearance together and even their partial amalgamation may be a feature of religious revivalism generally, not only in Israel. A militant, highly politicized, right-wing religious movement has come along with and feeds off a more widespread revival of traditional piety and Orthodox practice. Something like this has happened in India and Algeria as well.

Since both these versions of Judaism were born in statelessness, their political enactment in an actual state is often strident, confused, and contradictory. Their protagonists are at once fearful of the non-Jewish world and hostile to it, anxious and aggressive. They are opportunistically committed to the state, reliant on its military strength, eager to use its coercive power on their own behalf. But they are quick to deny the legitimacy of the state's elected and (even more) its judicial representatives whenever they don't like official policies. They are more committed to their religion than to their nation, or they are nationalists with a ghetto mentality, at once parochial and zealous, besieged and belligerent.

Who benefits from this kind of politics? Marxist analysis isn't of much help in this case. Israeli capitalists don't benefit from religious zealotry; the Tel Aviv bourgeoisie are immune to it and threatened by it. The rabbis do benefit; their authority is enhanced; and given their following, they are a social force, though with no particular class base. Right-wing populist politicians find new opportunities. The post-1967 settlers benefit greatly, at least in the short run, but they are the creation of zealotry, not its cause. No one else's position is likely to be improved or strengthened. Can Jewish zealots and traditionalists exercise effective power in the modern world, or sustain a modern economy, or negotiate with Israel's neighbors, or find a way to peace with the Palestinians? Can they reconcile rabbinic authority with democratic deliberation and disagreement? Can they govern justly in a state that includes large numbers of non-Jews and larger numbers of non-believing Jews?

My own view is that these questions cannot be successfully answered from a position of religious militancy; ultimately, the counterrevolution will fail, although the traditionalists and the zealots may play significant roles in coalition governments, and a modern state with antimodern ministers is a formula for trouble. How is such a thing possible, given the success of national liberation? In fact, Zionist responses to the eruption of messianism and the return of traditionalism have been surprisingly weak. Political reasons aside, the chief intellectual reason for the weakness is the double failure of cultural negation. On the one hand, the old religious culture was not overcome; on the other hand, the new secular culture isn't thick or robust enough to sustain itself by itself.

To explain the "return to pre-emancipation days," the literary and social critic Aharon Megged says simply: "Every vacuum . . . must fill up."[35] This isn't quite fair, since Zionist writers and activists did a great deal to fill the cultural space left by the negation of the exile. The new culture was partly a reflection of the history of the movement itself and the experience of its pioneers, but it also reached back to the Bible and outward to nineteenth- and twentieth-century liberationist ideologies. Arthur Hertzberg has said of Zionism that "its ultimate values derive from the general [European] milieu," but it none-theless produced its own ideas and institutions, heroes and holidays, ceremonies and celebrations, songs and dances. All these together dominated Israeli culture for a couple of generations.[36] The reproduction of secular Zionism has faltered badly in the past few decades, however, and Megged's claim that there isn't anything there has acquired greater currency than it deserves.

But even if a vacuum doesn't exist, the cultural air is thin, as I suggested in the first chapter; something is missing; there is a historical loss. A strong connection exists, I believe, between that loss and the radical negation with which Zionism began. M. J. Berdichevsky, one of the fiercest advocates of negation, a Jewish Nietzschean, saw the causal link with clarity. Writing sometime before 1900, he said of his own critical ideas: "They are powerful; they have the strength to undermine everything, to change everything . . . to call into question all the ancient values."

But, he said, "if they are the conquerors, I am the con-
quered . . . Sometimes I feel that I am killing myself."[37]

The secularists did not kill themselves; they still rule
over much of Israeli culture if not over Israeli politics. But
their hegemony is precarious these days. They can no
longer bridge the secular/religious dichotomy that is a
central effect of radical negation. "Secular" describes the
people for whom the exile has indeed been negated; "religious," those for whom it definitely hasn't been negated,
who sustain and now actively promote the old culture in
the new state. There are no middle terms of the sort that
hegemonic intellectuals ought to be able to invent, no
compromised versions of negation, no liberalized versions
of religion. Perhaps Zionist biblicism was intended as a
synthesis of the religion of the ancient Israelites with modern secularist ideology—the connection forged through
historical study, archaeology, exploration of the land, secular adaptations of biblical holidays (Passover as Israel's
first liberation; Hanukah as a celebration of religious freedom), and so on. But all that was artificial, given the history of the Jews. "The leap to the Bible," Gershom Scholem argued in a 1970 interview, "is purely fictitious, the
Bible being a reality that does not exist today."[38] In any
case, the leap was only to the most politically useful biblical texts (in the case of Hanukah, early postbiblical), and it

invited counterleaps to different texts. A line in Shakespeare's *Merchant of Venice* resonates with recent Israeli experience: "The devil can cite Scripture for his purpose."

The Bible is a Jewish text, and a critical engagement with it could, and sometimes does, produce interesting arguments. But I want to suggest an alternative to this Zionist search for a useful past. Perhaps the alternative could not have been realized in the history that I have just described, but it might still be relevant for the future. What national liberation required was a critical engagement with the postbiblical Jewish tradition—that is, with Judaism itself. Scholem argued that a "dialectic" of rebellion and continuity marked Zionism from the beginning.[39] The rebellion takes the form of secular negation (and a leap to the Bible); the continuity is embodied in traditional Judaism. These two are certainly contradictory, but they haven't been brought into a dialectical relation, in which each influences the other and the two are transformed in some interactive way. What sorts of moves from each of the two sides might make their interaction possible? I can speak only from the side of secular rebellion and try to answer half of that question: How might a critical engagement with the tradition strengthen liberationist— that is, Zionist—culture? In chapter 4, I will lay out a tentative response, and I will also suggest that this question has a close analogue in recent Indian debates about the future of Nehruvian secularism.

But first I need to deal with Marxist and postcolonial critics who deny that there is a paradox of national liberation, who insist that the question at which I have just arrived isn't the right question, and who argue that the strengthening of Zionist culture or Nehruvian secularism is not a desirable goal. I will take up that line of criticism in the next chapter.

THREE

The Paradox Denied

Marxist Perspectives

The paradox with which I began has to do with the tense relationship between liberators and the people they aim to liberate—and actually do liberate. The relationship simultaneously encompasses deep sympathy and deep hostility. Sympathy, because the liberators don't just resent the foreign rulers and hope to replace them; they really want to improve the everyday lives of the men and women with whom they identify: *their* people (the possessive pronoun is important). Hostility, because at the same time the liberators hate what they take to be the backwardness, ignorance, passivity, and submissiveness of those same people. They want to help their people by transforming them, by overcoming or modernizing their traditional religious beliefs and practices—to which many or most of them are firmly attached.

The position that I implicitly, and sometimes explicitly, defended in the first two chapters is one of sympathy for this transformative enterprise coupled with criticism of its harsher, more singular and absolute versions. I should add that in two of my three cases, India and Israel, the rule of the liberation militants in their new states was not particularly harsh. The massacres and ethnic cleansing brought on by the partition of British India and the expulsions that accompanied the Arab-Israeli War of 1948 lay in the past. Nehru's government ruled with force in Kashmir and in Nagaland and other provinces in India's northeast; Israel imposed military rule over the western Galilee and its mostly Arab inhabitants.[1] But by world standards, these were liberal regimes with opposition parties, a highly critical press, and free universities. Indeed, a contemporary Indian sociologist notes Nehru's "refusal to use the coercive powers of the state in hastening the [secularization] process." Nehru was too much a liberal on this view, or he was too optimistic about the decline of religion. "He invites comparison with Lenin and Ataturk," says this critic, "and, if you allow dictatorship, suffers by it."[2] Well, I don't "allow" dictatorship and have been hinting at a very different, perhaps exactly opposite, critique of the liberation militants: they didn't acknowledge the substantive seriousness and strength of their traditionalist opponents and begin a process of engagement and negotiation with them. But I agree that it is entirely appropriate to be skeptical about this critique. After all, those who did try to engage with the traditions of their people rather than simply negate them were not successful in any of the cases I am considering. They could not resolve the paradox of national liberation, nor could they ward off the religious revival.

Before asking again how one might deal with the paradox, I need to consider two alternative accounts of Indian national liberation, Marxist and postcolonial, which deny that there is a paradox to deal with. On these views, the aging militants of the liberation movements (in Israel and Algeria, too) should not be surprised by the religious revival, for they are its direct cause. Revivalist religion, an Indian friend said to me, is the "dark twin" of national liberation. The opposition on which I have focused is a mere squabble between social forces that are, whatever their militants and true believers think, world-historical allies.

The Marxist account holds that religious beliefs and the fiercely defended identities that these beliefs produce are examples of false consciousness, that they are not usefully engaged with the "real world" of contending social classes and don't serve the needs of oppressed men and women. The liberationists fail to overcome these beliefs and identities because their own nationalism is similar in form: it is also an example of false consciousness, it draws on the same primordial ideas and emotions, and it fails, like religion, to serve the needs of the oppressed. Whatever the pretended opposition of nationalism and religious revival, these two reinforce each other, and they make for a narrow, parochial, and chauvinist politics. Postcolonial writers, by contrast, see the two as specifically modern creations. They stress, with a kind of romantic nostalgia, the "'fuzzy,' syncretistic, reciprocal, and overlapping character of pre-modern religious identities" and argue that the monolithic and exclusive religions that foster zealotry are the products of colonial rule—which the liberationists do not challenge so much as perpetuate. Indian nationalists appropriate "characteristically Western forms of disciplinary power." That Hindu militants compete with them to exercise this power can't be surprising.[3]

I am going to focus mostly on the Marxist critique in this chapter, since I find it the more appealing, the more challenging, and the more usefully wrong of the two. It is also important to recognize that Marxist universalism is very close in spirit to the prevailing view among Western philosophers that both religion and nationalism are narrowly and dangerously parochial. The politics that follows from this intellectual closeness is socialist for the Marxists and liberal for most of the philosophers. Since I am sympathetic to both socialism and liberalism, I need to explain why national liberation is not an affront to either. This isn't an original or peculiar project; socialist and liberal writers before me have worked to reconcile universalist and nationalist commitments.[4]

I will say something about the postcolonial critique in the first part of chapter 4, although I won't be able to deal with it in any adequate way. Amartya Sen seems right to me when he notes that some postcolonial arguments "involve elaborate conceptual compositions and estimable intricacy of language and are not breathtakingly easy to penetrate (even armed with a dictionary of neologisms, on the one hand, and courage, on the other)."[5] My own argument will address only a simplified and, I hope, commonsensical version of postcolonialism.

The Marxist critique begins just as I began—with a nation whose members have adjusted to foreign rule, accepted their subordinate roles, and even found ways, especially religious ways, to legitimize their own subordination. Writers in the Indian academic journal *Subaltern Studies* have argued that there were strong undercurrents of resistance and sometimes actual rebellions: evasive and subversive behavior in the everyday world and occasional peasant jacqueries and millennialist uprisings.[6] But by and large the colonial rulers maintained their domination with remarkably small numbers of soldiers and police. Their subjects were mostly passive, quiescent, submissive. They fit the description given by the national liberation militants, except that nothing in their condition is peculiar to their nation. In fact, they are exactly like, or fundamentally similar to, subordinate men and women everywhere—and it is critically important that they come to recognize the similarity. The sense of oneself as the member of a subject people, writes Edward Said in *Culture and Imperialism*, is "the founding insight of anti-imperialist nationalism," but it will lead to chauvinism and xenophobia unless the individual member "sees his own history as an aspect of the history of *all* subjugated men and women."[7] The alternative account is a universalizing account, which denies that oppression has a national name. Indians are not oppressed as Indians, or Jews as Jews, or Algerians as Algerians. They are simply subject peoples, parts of a global proletariat. And it is a mistake to think that their liberation has to be, or can be, a national liberation.

Perry Anderson, the longtime editor of *New Left Review*, has developed the most subtle version of this argument in a comparison of countries and movements only a little different from my own—he deals with India, Israel, and Ireland. In these three countries, he writes,

the nationalist party that came to power after independence . . . distanced itself from the confessional undertow of the struggle without ever being able to tackle its legacy head on. In each case, as the ruling party gradually lost its luster, it was outflanked by a more extreme rival that had fewer inhibitions about appealing directly to the theological passions aroused in the original struggle. The success of these parties was due . . . to their ability to articulate openly what had always been latent in the national movement, but neither candidly acknowledged nor consistently repudiated.[8]

On this view, the liberators try to "distance themselves" from the religious commitments of their fellows, but they don't have the courage or, because of their nationalism, the capacity to do so openly, explicitly, and consistently. Religious passion remains latent and unchallenged in their nationalist project. In effect, the militants of national liberation create the modern nation in much the same way as the revivalists later on create a modernized religion: by evoking its primordial character, by searching for heroic moments in its history, and by insisting, at the same time, on the injuries it has suffered at the hands of conquerors and persecutors. While they are critical (but never sufficiently critical) of the actual culture of their people, they recover or invent a historic culture that they can celebrate. And all this brings with it the "undertow" of the old religion.

So the nation becomes the prison of its liberators, and fundamentalist religion turns out to be nationalism's secret double or, for Anderson, its unchosen but inevitable successor, claiming "with a certain justice," to be its legitimate heir. My friend's phrase "dark twin" isn't quite right, for national liberation on this view is as dark as religious revival. The two of them are equally parochial and exclusive; they lead inevitably to the creation of "others" who are excluded from the nation, treated as enemies, feared and hated; they give rise to a chauvinist and intolerant politics.[9]

Of course, the militants of national liberation have a different view of their project. Many of them can rightly insist that their repudiation of the old religion was, over many years, resolutely explicit and entirely consistent. And all of them argue that their aim is not the aggrandizement of their nation but equal membership in the society of nations and reciprocity with the "others." But insofar as they are nationalists—this is the alternative account—they cannot achieve these goals without mobilizing their own nation, and in practice that means appealing to blood ties, gut feelings, and irrational beliefs. The liberators imitate the believers they hope to defeat; they appropriate the religious themes of martyrdom and vindication-to-come; they set past and future glory against present humiliation. Whatever they say about their goals, the political struggle they begin is not simply aimed at independence, or equality, or religious freedom, but at triumph over ancient enemies, many of whom are also members of a different faith—infidels.

Anderson limits his argument to nationalist movements "in which religion played a central organizing role from the start, providing, so to speak, the genetic code of the movement."[10] The biological imagery is a mistake, as it always is in writing about politics, but I don't disagree with Anderson's effort to focus the argument. I am afraid, though, that many more cases than his three, or my three, will have to be included. Most national histories are entangled with religious histories. That's why the militants have to work so hard at disentanglement. That's what makes national liberation so problematic. Asked by André Malraux what his most difficult task after independence had been, Nehru replied at first piously and then more realistically: "Creating a just state by just means," he said, and then, "perhaps, too, creating a secular state in a religious country."[11]

That project is especially difficult after centuries of foreign rule and statelessness—for it is only the state that provides the necessary space within which lines can be drawn between religion and politics. In a deep sense, it is only states that can be secular. Wherever political authority takes statelike forms, its protagonists work hard to achieve independence from religious authority. The conflict between church and state is a prominent feature of medieval European politics—and of European politics in modern times. The conflict is another European export. Liberationists in India, Israel, and Algeria could certainly learn its importance by looking around their own countries, but it was helpful to know, as Nehru certainly knew, that they were fighting a battle that had been fought before.

The Marxist view of national liberation holds that secularists like Nehru weren't secular enough—couldn't be secular enough so long as they were also committed to the nation-state (and not, say, to a workers' state). Inevitably, the liberation militants summon up the religious zealots. For the militants, the zealotry is a shock; the conflict with the zealots is critical, even shattering. For their Marxist critics, by contrast, the conflict is only a surface phenomenon; the doctrinal differences are not deep, and the underlying parochialism of both sides and the passions it engenders are very much alike.

It follows that Gandhi's political use of Hindu motifs, his "unrestrained injection of religious discourse into political space," is not an exception to the general rule of national liberation; it is, in fact, an especially clear example of the general rule.[12] Only his pacifism is exceptional.

Yes, as V. S. Naipaul wrote, Gandhi "called up [India's] archaic religious emotions," but that is what all nationalists do, even when they think they are opposing religion. Those archaic religious emotions are closely connected to the archaic national emotions that are the necessary material of liberationist propaganda. In fact, the two sets of emotions are, in many cases, virtually identical. Hinduism as a unified and coherent world religion, standing with Christianity and Islam, may be an invention of the British; the opposition of Hindus and Muslims may, in part, be the consequence of imperial policy. It is still the case that Hindu beliefs and practices and Hindu understandings of defeat and oppression played a crucial role in Indian national mobilization—and they served at the same time to remind (Hindu) Indians that there was a Muslim conquest before the British conquest. Efforts to evoke the image of an independent India inevitably looked back to the time of a Hindu raj.

Many Hindu nationalists, in Nehru's time and later, were not religious at all. V. D. Savarkar, the chief ideologue of Hindutva, who invented the word, wrote a book defending the idea that Hindus, not Indians, were a nation and that Hinduism, in all its varieties, was simply the "culture" of the nation. But he also wrote that India was the Hindu "holy land," thus demonstrating, I suppose, Anderson's "undertow." India, according to Savarkar, was no one else's holy land: Muslim and Christian Indians had holy lands of their own, far away. Hindu beliefs and practices were signs of membership in a nation, which required sovereignty, and not membership in a religious community, which required only toleration. Or, rather, the nation and the religion were radically entangled. Savarkar imagined an inclusive Hindu community; he wanted to bring in Jains and Sikhs and to bring back men and women who had converted to Islam or Christianity. But they could come back only if they returned to the "culture" of Hinduism, which was in fact a religious culture.[13]

Ashis Nandy, one of the postcolonial critics of national liberation, is certainly right to point out that the Hindutva ideologues don't really like traditional Hinduism, which is "too diverse, feminised, irrational, unversed in the intricacies of the modern world, and too pantheistic, pagan, gullible, and anarchic to run a proper state."[14] They want a more muscular religion to go along with their nationalist project, but their project, unlike liberation, remains dependent on a religious base.

Theorists of Hindutva like Savarkar, and also the more radical M. S. Golwalkar, frequently compared themselves to the Zionists, who were also asserting the claim of a nation that was often described as a religious community. The difference is that the Jewish sense of peoplehood was clearer, at least to the Jews or to the greater number of them: *Am Yisrael*, the people of Israel, was the most common name for the Jews among the Jews themselves. The Zionists aimed to create a modern nation out of an ancient (and, they would have said, decadent) one, but the ingredients necessary to the creation already existed: not only a common history, culture, and law, all of which the Zionists wanted to transform, but also a pervasive sense of the importance of the commonality. Nationhood was a Zionist ambition, but it wasn't a Zionist fabrication; indeed, the strongest secular opponents of the Zionists, those who defended Diaspora Jewry and advocated autonomy in eastern Europe (and elsewhere), also believed in nationhood. Orthodox Jews, although they had a radically different understanding of the Jewish people, never doubted its existence. Reform Jews in the West claimed to be a religious community only, whose members were German or French or British nationals, but their gentile neighbors mostly did not agree. The idea of a Jewish nation was in no sense novel or surprising.[15]

Hindu nationhood, by contrast, was an ideological construction entirely unknown to most Hindus; even among its advocates it had a short history. In delineating this ideological nation and marking its boundaries, the Hindutva theorists could not avoid religious markers of a fairly extreme sort. Thus Golwalkar, in his 1938 description of a future Hindustan, wrote:

The non-Hindu people of Hindustan must either
adopt Hindu culture and languages . . . learn and
respect and hold in reverence the Hindu religion . . .
entertain no ideas but those of glorification of the
Hindu race and culture . . . In a word they must cease
to be foreigners; or they may stay in the country,
wholly subordinated to the Hindu nation, claiming
nothing, deserving no privileges, far less any prefer-
ential treatment—not even citizen rights.[16]

The line from this sort of thing to an overt religious
zealotry is easy to make out—not so the line from Congress nationalism, whose ideologues, like Nehru, insisted
that India's culture was "composite" or "syncretic" and
not simply Hindu. Not so the line from Labor Zionism
either, whose protagonists were not inclined to hold Judaism in reverence, let alone require everyone else to do
that. There are indeed nationalists and Orthodox zealots
today who would like the state of Israel to embody the
same radical entanglement of nation and religion that the
theorists of Hindutva advocate—so that Judaism would be
the sole criterion for citizenship and Jewish law would shape
state legislation. But it was a central aim of most Zionists
to separate what Savarkar and Golwalkar struggled to bring
together. They wanted a secular state in which religious
Jews would feel at home, as they had never felt in any of

their exilic homes, but which would also include nonreligious Jews and non-Jews as equal citizens.

Savarkar thought of himself as a man of the enlightenment, a secular rationalist, but he had, as Nandy writes, "paradoxically arrived at the conclusion that only religion could be an efficacious building block for nation- and state-formation in South Asia." His kind of nationalism was the dark twin of religious zealotry. But throughout his life, says Nandy, he "remained at the margin of Indian politics."[17] How then did he move posthumously into the center?

For the Marxist account of national liberation, that is not a hard question: the answer is that Nehru's politics was closer to Savarkar's than either of them would ever have admitted. I want to give that argument its due—in the Israeli and Algerian cases also. So let me acknowledge that the Jewish love of Zion, the original holy land, was a necessary foundation of Zionist politics. The militants of Labor Zionism, secularists all, could not help but evoke that religious emotion even if they agreed with Hillel Zeitlin that "the same tradition that burdens us in the Diaspora will burden us a thousand times more in *Eretz Yisrael*." The love of Zion made the Uganda project impossible, as I argued in the second chapter; it is powerfully expressed in "Hatikva," Israel's national anthem, which Arab citizens are loath to sing since it expresses a peculiarly Jewish longing for the "Land of Israel."

The case is the same in Algeria. The Arabs came to the Mahgreb as a conquering people, and Islam was the reason for the conquest and then the ideological foundation of Arab rule. Many centuries later, it was perhaps the crucial reason for Algerians to identify themselves as not-French and to resist the incorporation of Algeria into the French republic. The politically opportunistic commitment of the FLN to the "principles of Islam" may have been more consequential than the movement's leaders intended. Their retreat on the woman question certainly suggests what might be called a "natural" drift from national liberation to religious revival.

So the central claim of the Marxist account (with which many liberal philosophers would agree) is this: parochialism is parochialism, whether it calls itself national or religious. From a universalist standpoint, the secular and religious versions of Indian, Jewish, and Algerian nationalism are pretty much indistinguishable. They feed one another, and if the best intentions of the secular militants are frustrated, the frustration is their own work, the necessary consequence of their nationalist commitments. By contrast, the universalism of the alternative account derives from internationalist commitments, which are based on social classes and economic interests rather than on nations and religions.

These commitments are nicely illustrated by G. Aloysius, an Indian historian and social theorist, who argues that the nationalist movement, precisely because of its religious affinities, prevented the maturing of the masses and their "emergence . . . into a new interest-based political community." The much-vaunted campaign against untouchability, he writes, "reduced a total . . . struggle against ascriptive hierarchy to a nominal symbolic struggle for a minority of Untouchable castes."[18] It is certainly true that the caste system made, and still makes, class politics difficult in India, but there is little evidence that an uprising of all the Indian subaltern groups was waiting to happen but was diverted by Congress nationalists into a merely symbolic campaign against untouchability. Aloysius is repeating an older argument first made by M. N. Roy, the founder of the Indian Communist Party and its most distinguished intellectual (he was expelled from the party in 1928), that Gandhi's Non-cooperation Movement of 1920–22 had "killed a revolution." National liberation, Roy insisted, could be won only if Congress were willing to "mobilize the revolutionary energy of the toiling masses." I am afraid, however, that Aloysius's "total struggle" and Roy's "revolutionary energy" existed more in theory than in practice. Or, better, they should have existed, and they are evoked by these writers as if they actually did exist.[19] But any liberationist militant in the real world, counting on the political maturity of the toiling masses, would have ended up not with a social movement but with an isolated sect.

The Marxist project failed or, at least, has not yet succeeded. The liberationists have not been pushed aside by the emergence of the masses as a mature political force. Nor have they been replaced, in the absence of the masses, by the revolutionary vanguard of the global proletariat. And even if that replacement had occurred, the vanguard militants would have encountered the same problem that the liberationists did: they would have found themselves at war with the very people whose interests they claimed to advance. Indeed, their war might have been more intense since it wasn't only the religious feelings but also the national-cultural commitments of ordinary men and women that the vanguard militants could not or would not acknowledge.

Attempting to rally the people, Marxist internationalists would have appealed to universal principles rather than to "archaic" emotions. Theirs would have been a cosmopolitan rather than a parochial mobilization. In their politics, they would have cultivated a new solidarity of the oppressed across all the boundaries of nation and religion. Hindu and Muslim, Jew and Arab, Algerian and pied noir, would have found themselves working together, global allies against the global axis of capitalism and imperialism. Post-Marxist critics of nationalism still long for this global alliance.

It is an attractive vision, perhaps the most authentic representation of secularism and enlightenment. But it was never realized, and we need to reflect for a moment on the failure of the cosmopolitan revolutionaries—and on the success, however qualified, of national liberation. The revolutionaries were not just unlucky. Nowhere in the world did proletarian internationalism succeed, even for a brief time, in displacing national identification. Marx may have been right about the importance of class interest, but he was certainly wrong about the relative appeal of class-based and nation-based politics. Foreign rule was everywhere experienced as a form of *national* oppression, in whose miseries all social classes shared; and opposition to foreign rule cut across class lines. Even when opposition was initiated and led by upper- or middle-class groups, workers and peasants eventually joined in. A cosmopolitan liberation movement may or may not come after the triumph of national liberation—that is still an open question. But it has never come first, and efforts to make it come first do not bring anything like liberation.

Nor do the liberation militants willingly stop short of political independence and a sovereign nation-state. The Austro-Marxists made one of the most interesting attempts to accommodate nationalist aspiration within an internationalist framework when they acknowledged the value of national culture while denying the necessity of sovereignty. Just as the national liberationists had a goal, namely, a state like other states, so, too, did these revolutionary intellectuals have a goal, namely, an empire unlike other empires. They were opposed to nationalism as a political ideology, and they favored the incorporation of many nations into a single political unit. This was exactly what the old empires had achieved, but imperial incorporation had also meant subordination to a single dominant power—the Ottomans, the British, the French, the Romanovs, the Hapsburgs—whereas the Austro-Marxists aimed at an empire without dominance and without subordination.[20]

Their structural model was the multinational empire that they lived in: Austria-Hungary. They didn't want to break up this political unit, but they did mean to transform it by granting equal citizenship to all its inhabitants and "cultural autonomy" to the previously subject nations. "Each national association," as John Schwarzmantel has explained, "would regulate its own affairs through nationally separated and self-governing administrative units." National minorities in "mixed" areas "would be safeguarded through their constitution as public bodies with definite rights."[21] But self-government would not interfere with economic planning or compete with the democratic state. When Otto Bauer wrote that "socialist society will undoubtedly present a variegated picture of national associations . . . and territorial bodies; it will be as different from the centralized, atomistic constitution of present-day states as from the equally varied and complex organization of medieval society," he did not mean to deny the working class its singular triumph or call into question the building of a socialist economy. The "variegated picture" would be cultural and religious in character: nations would be "encouraged to develop autonomously and to enjoy freely their national culture," but they would not control their own economies; they would not have their own police.[22]

Bauer's is another attractive vision. Looking at eastern Europe today, I find it hard to deny that a democratized Austro-Hungarian Empire, with cultural autonomy for all the subject nations, would have been a better political outcome than the one that national liberation militants (or, better, nationalist militants) produced. Similarly, a democratized version of imperial India, with cultural autonomy for Muslims and Hindus, as well as other groups, might have avoided the disaster of partition—which would certainly have been better than what national liberation produced. The only problem is that these better outcomes did not have anything like the necessary political support. They didn't appeal to the traditionalists, although autonomy might have served them well. And they didn't appeal to the liberationists, who had more particular projects in mind. But what was probably most important in the failure of Marxist internationalism was the widely shared belief that only sovereignty guaranteed the cultural survival of national and religious groups (and perhaps also the physical survival of their members), and only sovereignty could bring full equality in the already existing society of states.

From the failure of internationalism in practice, however, it doesn't follow that the theoretical critique of national liberation is wrong. I suppose that the obligatory "unity of theory and practice" requires us to be skeptical now about Marxist internationalism: if the practice has failed, then the theory should be in trouble. But the critique of national liberation is also a moral critique, which holds that the liberationists share responsibility for all the "dark" features of contemporary nationalism, including those that are marked by religious zeal. Can this be right, given that so many of the national liberation militants were so fiercely antireligious? It is certainly true that secularism was something new for Indians, Jews, and Algerians; the separation of religion and politics was an artifact of liberationist politics—hence artificial. Any effort to find "liberationist" themes in the history of these peoples, moments of independence, activism, solidarity, and self-sacrifice, would inevitably draw on religiously inflected events and beliefs. The collective goals of the national liberation movements overlapped with and were often expressed in the language of religious hopes and dreams. All that is true; I have already acknowledged that Gandhi was not the only one to evoke "archaic" emotions.

On the other hand, secularist commitments did make a difference, and it is important to focus on that difference in order to recognize the value of the liberationist project to its militants and to argue, as I will in the last chapter of this book, that the project is worth completing. So, consider once more the Jewish belief that the Messiah will bring the exiled people home to the Land of Israel. This ingathering became a central Zionist goal, but now it was reconceived as a political project, subject to all the normal vicissitudes of politics, requiring organization, fundraising, diplomacy, compromise, and possibly (the subject of harrowing debates) the use of force. The idea of waiting for divine deliverance was finally rejected, and that idea lay at the heart of exilic Judaism.[23]

The case is the same with the religious idea of "settling the land." The Zionist maxim "Another dunam, another goat" is not only a prosaic version of this idea; it is also a transformed version, focused now on human effort and open to the necessity of compromise and limit. The religious idea does not admit of dividing the land, but dividing the dunams is a real possibility. Of course, religious revival produces its own transformations: when Jewish zealots entered into the practical work of settling the land after the Six-Day War in 1967, they were not waiting for the Messiah; rather, they were (in the old religious language) "forcing the end." But they acted with a sense that the end was near, that they were on the brink of messianic times, that the success of their work was divinely guaranteed— all of which made the ideas of compromise and limit inconceivable to them.

The case is the same again with the advocacy by some FLN militants of "Islamic socialism"—which turned out, when theory gave way to practice, to be Marxist state socialism decorated with a few lines from the Qur'an. The adjective "Islamic" did nothing to modify the noun. The "social state" that all the FLN manifestos promised challenged the traditional Muslim acceptance of private property and failed to require the submission of the Algerian people to shari'a law. So the religious revivalists of the 1980s did not appeal, as Anderson's argument might suggest, to what was "latent" in the idea of a social state or Islamic socialism; they rejected both.[24]

One can argue that the liberationist project made the zeal of the revival possible—historically that is certainly true—just as one might rightly say that the Enlightenment made the counter-Enlightenment possible. But I doubt that it is morally right to blame the liberationists for the zealots. It would be a mistake to ignore the difference between the two ways of settling the Land of Israel. Similarly, it would be a mistake to ignore the difference between Gandhi and Nehru's critique of untouchability, however incomplete it was, and the Hindu nationalists' defense of the "functional organization of society." Hindutva isn't implicit in and doesn't follow from the incompleteness of the Nehruvian critique. It is more accurate to say that it follows from the (partial) success of national liberation. As Thomas Blom Hansen has argued, Hindutva is a conservative reaction against a broad "democratic transformation of both the political field and the public culture in post-colonial India."[25] I think he means an egalitarian transformation. In fact, Hindu nationalists have made good use of democracy, which has brought their followers, previously passive, inarticulate, and committed to the routines of the old religion, into political life. Recall Bhargava's explanation for the rise of Hindu nationalism: the propensity of representative democracy "to encourage ethno-religious political mobilization." It is another sign of the paradox of national liberation that the mobilization it made possible can be and (in part) has been turned against social and gender equality—against liberation, in fact.

The contrasting politics of liberationist militants and

religious zealots might be described in another way. All three of these national liberation movements claimed that they were going to create a democratic state and a just legal order. And in all three of them, democracy and justice were generally understood in standard, that is, European ways. (In Algeria, the one-party state was understood in east European ways.) I won't immediately say that democracy and justice are universal ideals, but that is what most of the militants believed. They imitated the values of the European Enlightenment, which are expressed in universal terms and which certainly set the militants against their own people's parochialism. They were nationalists who wanted their nations to measure up to principles established elsewhere—indeed, their commitment to those principles was probably stronger than that of their Marxist critics. (Again, the Algerians are a partial exception here.)

The liberationist militants wanted to join the society of states, which in its origins was a European society but in its ambitions a global society. They wanted, as the Zionists said, to be "normal." By contrast, the religious zealots want to be different. They don't aim at a state like all the other states; they want a state shaped by their own interpretation or reinterpretation of a particular religious tradition. That's why they resist what they call the imitative discourse of democracy and human rights, invoking instead Hindu culture and "Asian values" or Jewish or Islamic law.

The same contrast can be illustrated even with regard to the treatment of the new minorities created by national liberation—Muslims in India, Arabs in Israel, Berbers in Algeria—where the Marxist and universalist critique of nationalism is seemingly strongest. I have focused up until now on the tense relationship of the liberation militants to their own people, but one of the sources of this tension is the commitment of the militants to equality for other peoples. For these "others" were often the objects of traditional religious (and, later on, nationalist) disparagement; in practice or in principle, they were condemned to a subordinate position. How would they fare after independence had been won?

The liberationists were committed first of all to the revival of their own nation, but in the Indian case, this nation was conceived from the beginning to include both Hindus and Muslims. Congress militants rejected Mohammed Ali Jinnah's claim that the Muslims constituted a nation of their own just as they rejected the claims of Hindu nationalists. Their state was meant to include only one Indian nation, but given the "composite" character of that nation, it was also meant to be a broadly inclusive state. Similarly, the states envisioned by Labor Zionists and the FLN were broadly inclusive, so members of the revived nation would share citizenship with non-members (like the Arabs in Israel) and with newly perceived minorities within the nation (like the Berbers in Algeria). I can't argue that any of the liberationists were successful in their inclusiveness; like all other left political movements in world history, they fell short. But I do want to argue that their original commitments, their political programs, were significantly different from those of the religious nationalists who came later. Those programs are important because they set up the ongoing critique of what national liberation accomplished and what it didn't accomplish. (Consider how the line about equality in the American Declaration of Independence set up the critique of the slave system that the revolutionaries refused to abolish; that line was still central to the work of civil rights activists in the 1960s.)

I will take up the Algerian case first. The FLN was committed from the beginning to a unitary state, with full equality for all its citizens. The Soummam Platform singled out Europeans and Jews as the future minorities that most needed to be reassured and accommodated. Although Berbers (chiefly from Kabylia) figured significantly in the leadership of the FLN and in the drafting of the platform, nothing was said there or, so far as I can tell, anywhere else about autonomy or linguistic equality for the Berber community—which turned out to be the most

important minority in the new state.[26] Once independence was won, and almost all the Europeans and Jews
were gone, the FLN government, first Ben Bella's and then
Boumedienne's, launched a fierce Arabization campaign,
a rejection of liberation for the sake of a straightforward
nationalism. The result was a brief uprising in Kabylia
and then, almost twenty years later, in the 1980s, a "Berber Spring," the beginning of an ongoing agitation for
state recognition of the language, culture, and history of
the Berber people.[27]

The FLN in power has steadily resisted this agitation.
But the liberation movement that it once was still has a
voice in Algerian politics: it is represented by militants
who found themselves in prison or in exile in the years
after 1962 and who continued to fight for a secular democracy. Fanon died of leukemia in 1961, and so wasn't
among them, as he might have been. Hocine Ait Ahmed,
one of the Berbers among the Historic Nine, was perhaps
the best spokesman for an ongoing liberationist politics.
He led the Front of Socialist Forces (FFS), a national political party that draws its support mostly from Kabylia.
Ait Ahmed went into opposition and into exile soon after
independence was won, when he dissented from the creation of a one-party state. In later years, he defended, with
considerable courage, a secular, pluralist, and democratic
politics. In the local elections of 1990 and the national

elections of 1991, when the Islamists swept the country, Kabylia remained a secular stronghold and voted strongly for the FFS.[28]

During the colonial years, the French touted the Berbers, in contrast to the Arabs, as almost-Europeans, the natural carriers of French culture in Algeria. I do not want to play that game. Many secular nationalists and democrats among Algerian Arabs, who can plausibly claim to descend from the original FLN, have set themselves against Islamist radicalism. In the drafting of the secular Soummam Platform, however, "the initiative lay . . . with the Kabyles [Berbers] as opposed to the Arabs," and in the years after 1962, the arabizing FLN regime, from whose leading positions Berbers were excluded, was not a force for liberation—not for women, as we have seen, and not for minorities.[29] Still, the state the FLN created was secular, and if it is ever replaced by an Islamic state, women will surely be worse off and the Berbers probably so. The Berbers are good Muslims (in the twelfth century, they were the Islamists of North Africa and Spain), but the ethnicity they celebrate is, after all, pre-Islamic.

Labor Zionists in power did better than the FLN in avoiding authoritarianism and brutality, but they, too, failed to live up to their egalitarian commitments. The state they created in May of 1948 was a Jewish state, but at the same time a secular state, with the rights of national and religious minorities guaranteed in the Declaration of Independence. Israel took over without significant change the millet system put in place by the Ottomans and maintained by the British. Arab Christians and Muslims have their own family courts, conducted in their own language, whose judges rule in accordance with their own religious law, just as the Jewish judges do. But this egalitarian arrangement, which owes more to enlightened imperialism than to national liberation (the secular liberationists don't regard the religious millets as a benefit for anyone), had no parallel in the society or the economy, where the commitment to equality was mostly ignored. Discrimination and neglect have been common features of the state's dealings with its Arab minority, although I think it is fair to say that within Israel proper the worst forms of abuse have been avoided. Arab political parties function freely, and a remarkably high number of Arab citizens vote in Israeli elections (Jews vote in larger numbers). It makes little sense to claim that religious zealotry in Israel today follows naturally from the nationalism of the Labor Zionists. It follows instead, as in India, from the democracy that the Labor Zionists created and then from their failure to produce a strong and coherent secular culture to go with that democracy. The zealots represent the return of what was only incompletely "negated." Their opposition to equality for the "others" isn't a continuation of an earlier Zionist politics but a repudiation of it or, at least, of its dominant version.[30]

Here is David Ben-Gurion speaking in late 1947, after the United Nations' vote for partition, to a meeting of Mapai, the political party that ruled Israel for its first three decades.

We must think in terms of a state, in terms of in-dependence, in terms of full responsibility for ourselves—and for others. In our state there will be non-Jews as well, and all of them will be equal citi-zens, equal in everything without any exception, that is, the state will be their state as well. The attitude of the Jewish state to its Arab citizens will be an impor-tant factor—though not the only one—in building good neighborly relations with the Arab states. The striving for a Jewish-Arab alliance requires us to fulfill several obligations which we are obliged to do in any event: full and real equality, de jure and de facto, of all the state's citizens, gradual equalization of the eco-nomic, social, and cultural standard of living of the Arab community with the Jewish community, recog-nition of the Arabic language as the language of the Arab citizens in the administration, courts of justice, and above all, in schools; municipal autonomy in villages and cities, and so on.[31]

Other Israeli politicians took very different positions from the one announced here. But this is an authoritative statement from the future prime minister addressed to the inner circle of his own party. We can take it as a liberationist vision of a state at peace with its neighbors. The invasion of the new state in 1948 by five Arab armies must count as one of the reasons, perhaps the crucial reason, why none of the governments over which Ben-Gurion presided lived up to the commitments he described. The equality he promised has never been realized in the nearly seven decades of Israel's history. But it is a matter of real importance that equality was for Ben-Gurion, as it was for the Algerian authors of the Soummam Platform, consistent with and even required by national liberation. For it is not required by, nor is it consistent with, the traditional religion or the religious nationalism that came later.

Before turning in the next chapter to the Indian debate about these issues, in which postcolonial writers have played a major part, let me stop here to quote from a speech and a letter that closely parallel Ben-Gurion's 1947 talk. The speech was delivered at the inaugural session of the Indian constituent assembly, where the newly created state's Constitution was drafted. The speaker was Rajendra Prasad, president of the assembly and later the first president of India; he was responding to the boycott of the assembly by members of the Muslim League.

We who are present in the House cannot forget even
for a moment that many of the seats are vacant at this
meeting. Our brethren of the Muslim League are not
with us, and their absence increases our responsibility.
We shall have to think at each step, What would they
have done if they had been here? We hope they will
come and take their place. But if unfortunately these
seats continue to remain unoccupied, it will be our
duty to frame a constitution which will leave no room
for complaint from anybody.[32]

The letter was written by Nehru to his newly appointed
ministers three months after partition:

We have a Muslim minority who are so large in
numbers that they cannot, even if they want to, go
anywhere else. This is a basic fact . . . Whatever the
provocations from Pakistan and whatever the indigni-
ties and horrors inflicted on non-Muslims there, we
have got to deal with this minority in a civilized man-
ner. We must give them the security and the rights of
citizens in a democratic state. If we fail to do so, we
shall have a festering sore which will eventually poison
the whole body politic and probably destroy it.[33]

The promises made in these texts extend beyond the
writing of the Constitution and the first years of statehood,

and like other liberationist promises, they remain unful-
filled. Muslim Indians have many legitimate complaints;
the sore festers. But I need to insist again that while national liberation may have its own pathologies, these are
not the same as or the source of the pathologies of contemporary politicized religion and religious nationalism.

The proving ground for every national liberation movement is the nation or the ethnic or religious group that
comes next: the Jews are tested by the Palestinians, the
Algerian Arabs by the Berbers, and the Indians by the
Muslims in their largely Hindu nation-state. Right now,
none of the three nations is scoring very high. The three
minority groups testify, nonetheless, to the strength of
the liberationist project by their imitation of it. Like self-
determination, liberation is a reiterative process: each
collective self must determine itself; each nation must
liberate itself. The proletarian revolution predicted by
Marxist writers may free all humanity at one go, but national liberation is always partial and particular. These
people free themselves, and other people, looking on, are
invited to do the same. So Labor Zionism doesn't produce religious zealotry; we might better say that its most
authentic product is the Palestinian national liberation
movement. Similarly, the Berber Spring is the most authentic product of FLN politics. And similarly again, liberationist and feminist movements inside India's Muslim

community are the product of India's composite democracy. If you are in favor of this kind of liberation—of peoples or nations or religious groups—you must be in favor of its repetitions. It would be morally inconsistent, as well as foolish, to imagine that the process stops with me, or with you and me, or with us.

The pathologies of religious zealotry, by contrast, do not derive from an inconsistent application of Hindu, Jewish, or Muslim doctrine but rather from a passionate consistency. If all these religious movements wanted was toleration for themselves, then they would be much like nations seeking liberation, and they would be bound, if not by the rule of reiteration, then by the rule of reciprocity: I will tolerate you if you will tolerate me. But toleration is not what the zealots want. They aim in each of my three cases to create a state that is entirely their own. The passion they bring to this effort is obviously a response to national liberation, but it is also radically different from it.

FOUR

The Future of National Liberation

I

If I insist on the strong opposition of secular national liberation to religious revivalism, if I deny their secret kinship and refuse to recognize the zealots as the necessary heirs of the liberators, then I must face once again the paradox of liberation and address the question it poses: Why have the leaders and militants of secular liberation not been able to consolidate their achievement and reproduce themselves in successive generations? Over the past several decades, Indian intellectuals and academics have been debating this question in its local version: "Why is it," one of them asks, "that the Nehruvian vision of a secular India failed to take hold?"[1] A leading figure in the recent debates is Ashis Nandy, whose work I have already cited, a longtime critic of both secular nationalism and Hindutva—the "disowned doubles of each other." In an article entitled "The Politics of Secularism and the Recovery of Religious Toleration," Nandy evokes a premodern, pluralist, and tolerant Hinduism ("fuzzy" and syncretistic), which, he says, the militants of national liberation ignored and suppressed. Their secular and modern radicalism produced a pathological reaction, which is revivalist and also modern; the modernism is shared. Having learned from Western theories of statecraft, the partisans of liberation and the partisans of religious revival are equally willing to use the power of the modern state against their opponents.[2]

So Nandy's "critique of Hindu nationalism," writes the philosopher Akeel Bilgrami, "is intended to be of a piece with the critique of Nehruvian secularism." Hindutva, "itself the product of modernity, owes its very existence to the oppositional but at the same time internal dialectical relation it bears to . . . secularism."[3] This isn't a Marxist, internationalist critique but rather an anti-modernist (or anti-Western) critique, and it has attracted wide support in India from writers, some of whom might best be identified as latter-day Gandhians; others are postmodernists and postcolonialists. Nandy argues that Gandhi's political use of Hindu motifs was justified because his Hinduism was authentic—that is, "located . . . in traditions outside the ideological grid of modernity" and therefore unavailable for parochial political mobilizations. By contrast, Hindutva is radically inauthentic. Nandy writes mockingly about the RSS, a paramilitary Hindu nationalist group:

> Whatever the revivalist Hindu may seek to revive, it is not Hinduism. The pathetically comic martial uniform of khaki shorts, which the RSS cadres have to wear, tells it all. Modeled on the uniform of the colonial police, the khaki shorts . . . identify the RSS as the illegitimate child of Western colonialism.

Nandy has similar things to say about the Nehruvian state, which took upon itself, he writes, the "same civilizing mission that the colonial states had once taken upon themselves vis-à-vis the ancient faiths of the subcontinent."[4]

That last point is certainly true; it is another example of the paradox of national liberation, but not one that necessarily carries the condemnation that Nandy intends. In 1829, for example, the British banned the sati—the ritual immolation of a Hindu widow on her husband's funeral pyre—and, after independence, the new Indian government reiterated the ban, acting out, I suppose, the "same civilizing mission." By contrast, Hindu revivalists and fundamentalists have spoken out in defense of sati, and in this case they don't appear to be inauthentic.[5] Indeed, the difficulty with Nandy's position, as his critics have pointed out, is that, however pluralist, tolerant, and "fuzzy" Hinduism may have been, it was also hierarchical and oppressive—and especially oppressive to women. The rise of Hindutva is as much a response to the egalitarianism of the liberationists as to their secularism. The hegemony of the Brahmans, the comforts of caste, and the traditional constraints on the life of women—all these are closer to the heart of the revival, and probably closer to the heart of the premodern religion, than is religious pluralism. For democrats and liberals, then, the ancient faith isn't and shouldn't be on the political agenda.

Nor should we be too quick to condemn the impact of Western modernity and of Western liberalism on Indian society. The "civilizing mission" was certainly hypocritical, an ideology for imperialism, but it was also sometimes a useful prod to local activists. As R. C. Dutt, one of the first presidents of the Indian National Congress, wrote in the early years of nationalist agitation: "The right of the *ryots* [peasants] to be educated, to be freed from the trammels of ignorance, to be saved from the oppression of *zamindars* [landed aristocrats]—such ideas have invariably emanated from our rulers and not from us."[6] More recently, Sumit Sarkar, in a Marxist critique of postcolonial studies, has pointed out that late-nineteenth- and early-twentieth-century lower-caste protests and movements for women's rights "quite often . . . tried to utilize Western ideologies and colonial law, justice, and administration as major resources."[7] These were "resources" not readily available in the indigenous (Hindu or Muslim) culture.

As I have argued in previous chapters, national liberation is the work of men and women who learned a great deal from their imperial rulers and used what they learned in the interests of liberation; they struggled simultaneously against imperial rule and against many of their own people's most revered customs and practices. The liberationists "retained the structures of the imperial state" because they believed, in the words of Dipesh Chakrabarty, one of the leading postcolonial writers, in an "Enlightenment rationalism" that "requires as its vehicle the modern state and its accompanying institutions—the instruments of governability, in Foucault's terms."[8] But if Chakrabarty means this critically, it is hard to see his point. What other instrument of governability (or of non-governability) could liberate the untouchables, end the ban on intercaste marriage, lift long-established restraints on the lives of women, and protect religious minorities? The new national state did each of these things in radically incomplete ways. But that statement is the beginning of a very different critique from the one the postcolonialists are making.

The statist commitment implicit in national liberation and the opposition of the liberationists to the customs of their people were too abstract, writes Aditya Nigam, a colleague of Nandy's at the Center for the Study of Developing Societies in New Delhi. It is as if the goal of the liberationists was not a "new Indian man," as they claimed, but a universal citizen of a universal state. The liberationist project had no concrete cultural content, Nigam argues, so it turned out to be a front for the continued domination of Brahmin elites, and its defenders were unable to offer significant resistance to the ideologists of Hindutva.[9] This argument is an Indian version of Aharon Megged's explanation for the failures of Zionist secularism and the rise of religious zealotry: "Every vacuum . . . must fill up." It isn't a fair argument in the Indian (or the Israeli) case: in the early years of independence, the Congress-dominated government undertook a massive educational effort on behalf of the new Constitution. Nehru and his friends energetically expounded and defended the liberal values they were trying to realize.

So Nandy may be right to claim that the problem with Nehruvian secularism wasn't that it was too abstract but rather that it was too rigidly ideological, too absolute in its challenge to Hindu (and Muslim) traditionalism. It is the absolutism of secular negation that best accounts for the strength and militancy of the religious revival. A number of Nandy's critics have also made this argument, and I want to look a little longer at their suggestions for dealing with Hindutva and its defenders. I will then ask whether the religious revival in Israel can be addressed in a similar way.

The critical error of Nehru's politics, according to Bilgrami, was that his secularism was "Archimedean" rather than "negotiated." By this Bilgrami means that "secularism stood outside the substantive arena of political commitments."[10] Remember Archimedes' boast that he could move the universe if only he could stand somewhere outside it. For the national liberationists, secularism was an external standpoint from which Indian society could be transformed. The secularist project didn't emerge from society itself; it wasn't the product of internal arguments and negotiations. As Nigam writes, Hindu (and Muslim) orthodoxy was "never defeated in open battle in society at large." And the reason that secularism wasn't negotiated or openly fought for, Bilgrami claims, is that Nehru and his associates were unwilling "to acknowledge the existence of [religious] communities and communitarian commitments."[11]

Why the unwillingness? The question requires us to recognize a deep tension in the liberationist position—a tension common, I think, to the two other national liberation movements. On the one hand, Nehru did not believe that the religious communities had a future. Religious belief, or at least its more fervent and "superstitious" versions, would "vanish at the touch of reality." After independence, Nehru predicted, there would be class conflicts but no religious conflicts "except insofar as religion itself expressed some vested interest"—he meant some economic interest. We have to wonder what India he had "discovered." Martha Nussbaum is certainly right to argue that Nehru "took religion far too lightly."[12] But, in fact, his faith in the decline of faith was, as I've already argued, widely shared. At the same time, Nehru knew very well the strength of both Hinduism and Islam, and he certainly understood the near identity of the caste and economic hierarchies. So his refusal to recognize the religious communities wasn't determined only by secular blindness but also by secular fear: he worried that recognizing them would strengthen them.. I suppose that these two views can be held simultaneously: religious identity is a clear and present danger whereas secularization, however inevitable, lies somewhere in the future. Still, they are different views, and in the Indian case the difference was acted out in a special way.

On the assumptions that the erosion of belief was well begun and could be speeded up and that vested interests had to be confronted, the new Indian state set out to reform Hindu laws and practices. The Constitution, written immediately after independence, abolished untouchability (Article 17) and banned discrimination on the basis of religion or caste (Article 15). Over the next decade, Parliament established a single code of personal law for all Hindu citizens. The parliamentary leaders of the dominant party, the Indian National Congress, acted with a slowness and reluctance that infuriated Ambedkar, the minister of justice, but they acted. The new code permitted intercaste marriage, legalized divorce, prohibited polygamy, gave daughters the same inheritance rights as sons, and much more.[13] The aim of the liberationists, Partha Chatterjee writes, was "to initiate a process of rational interpretation of religious doctrine."[14] In fact, what they were doing was denying that much of what was traditionally understood as religious doctrine was "religious." According to the new Constitution, every community had the right "to manage its own affairs in matters of religion." But state officials insisted on a narrow definition of religion—or, rather, on a narrow definition of Hinduism. "I do not understand," Ambedkar wrote, "why religion should be given [a] vast expansive jurisdiction so as to cover the whole of life." Religion properly encompassed belief and worship; everything else fell within the jurisdiction of the state. "After all," Ambedkar continued, "what are we having this liberty for?" The point of independence was "to reform our social system, which is so full of inequalities, discrimination, and other things which conflict with our fundamental rights."[15]

All this was said with regard to Hinduism. For what were probably good reasons, there was no similar effort to restrict the reach of Islam and establish a rationalized system of personal law for the Muslim minority. Nehru and his associates were not ready to challenge the strength of Islamic belief and the authority of shari'a. They probably feared that any such challenge would be regarded as religious persecution. For the majority, then, there would be liberation; for the minority, there would be religious liberty—with Islam allowed precisely the "vast expansive jurisdiction" that Ambedkar was so eager to deny to Hinduism. In effect, there were no negotiations with either religious community; state officials decided to reform Hindu law top-down and to tolerate Muslim law.[16] From the liberationist standpoint, this approach was greatly to the advantage of the Hindus. The socialist leader J. B. Kripalani argued that if the members of Parliament "single out the Hindu community for their reforming zeal, they cannot escape the charge of being communalists in the sense that they favor the [Hindus] and are indifferent to the good of the Muslims."[17] Hindu traditionalists made exactly the opposite charge, claiming that it was the Muslims who were being favored. In any event, top-down reform was only partially successful, so the favoritism was limited.

When India wrote its Constitution, Harold Isaacs reports, the untouchables became ex-untouchables by law, but they remained untouchables in fact. He provides a grim account of the life of the ex-untouchables in the early 1960s and adds in a 1973 postscript that not much had changed. Since then, an extensive program of affirmative action has opened new opportunities to younger members of what has come to be called, at the insistence of ex-untouchable militants, the Dalit ("oppressed") community. Hindutva is in part a reaction to the special treatment (reserved offices and welfare benefits) accorded to both the ex-untouchables and the lowest castes—a practice that has the effect of maintaining caste lines, since the people who claim special treatment "have to be properly sorted out and identified." At the same time, however, affirmative action threatens the traditional caste hierarchy.[18]

These are the ambiguities of liberation. They are perhaps especially clear in the case of Hindu and Muslim women: the former are the beneficiaries of the new civil code; the latter are still ruled by Islamic personal law. In a famous court case (Shah Bano) in 1985, the judges, acting on good liberationist principles, sought to extend the protection of the civil code to a divorced Muslim wife, but Parliament undid the decision with a new Muslim Women Act (1986). Who is being favored here? From the standpoint of Hindu nationalists, the new legislation was another example of the Indian state and the Congress party bending over backward to favor the Muslim minority, which was (again) allowed to maintain its traditional practices. By contrast, the All India Democratic Women's Association and other feminist groups, the true heirs of national liberation, insisted rightly that the new law was no favor to Muslim women. In March 1986, thirty-five women's organizations, including Muslim groups, joined together to demonstrate for a uniform secular code, which was the original promise of Nehru and his associates.[19]

I cannot pursue these issues any further; my knowledge of Indian history and politics doesn't reach to their complexities. I do, however, want to insist again that through all the compromises and confusions of political practice since 1947, it is still possible to mark clearly the differences between secular liberation and both traditional and revivalist religion. I suspect that the differences are clearest with regard to the subordination of women. The demand for gender equality poses the greatest challenge to traditional religion and is probably the most important cause of revivalist zealotry in all three of my cases. Certainly the members of the All India Democratic Women's Association, whose name suggests a national project, are in no sense the twins or the secret doubles of the Hindutva militants. Nor does Nehru's decision in the 1940s to allow religious liberty to the Muslim minority in the field of family law make him a twin of Muslim traditionalists, despite the happiness of the mullahs with the legal recognition of shari'a. Both these pairs—democratic women and Hindutva militants, Nehruvian liberals and Muslim traditionalists—are long-term political opponents. By what means should this opposition be pursued? What do Indian critics of Nehru's "Archimedean" politics mean when they call for a "negotiated" secularism?

In October 2004, the socialist magazine *Janata* reported on a conference in New Delhi on the condition of Muslim women; the conferees included feminist activists and (male) members of the Muslim Personal Law Board. Naturally, the two groups disagreed, but what was most interesting was that "numerous women participants argued . . . from within an Islamic paradigm, quoting verse after verse from the Qur'an and citing traditions attributed to the Prophet to [make] their case for gender justice." These women were a new force, says the *Janata* reporter; they had the "moral authority that feminists who are seen as alienated from their societies and traditions lack."[20]

The same claim can be made for the members of Women Living Under Muslim Laws (WLUML), a feminist organization founded in the 1980s by women from a number of Muslim majority countries, including Algeria, whose work has reached to India, where the Muslims are a (very large) minority.[21] The members of WLUML are both religious and secular, and one of their central goals is to provide reinterpretations of Muslim laws relating to the status of women. The plural form ("laws") is important to their project. They insist that there are different understandings and different enactments of what is always called Qur'anic law, not a single authoritative version delivered by learned men, as religious zealots insist. The plural form means that women can join the argument; and by joining the argument rather than standing outside it, they hope to win at least a hearing from religious Muslims, men and women alike. If they are learned, as many of them are, they can also be authoritative.

Amartya Sen lays claim to the same kind of moral authority for democrats and pluralists when he argues that the ideas of public debate and respect for religious difference have roots in ancient Indian thought. He provides many examples.[22] His argument is different from Nandy's, although some of his examples might serve them both. Sen claims that important modern ideas aren't modern inventions; they were expressed long ago, though in different idioms. They are part of a common heritage that may have to be selectively rejected but that can also be selectively reclaimed—and because selectivity is possible, Western ideas about liberty and equality can be naturalized in India. It may well be true that the best arguments for gender justice and for democratic pluralism are secular and philosophical in character. But philosophy doesn't rule the day here; the best moral and political arguments are ones that derive from or connect with the inherited culture of the people who need to be convinced. Engagement with that culture is what Nehru's critics mean by "negotiation." They argue that secularism in the West derives from a political negotiation with Protestant Christianity, so they imagine internal arguments that might produce Hindu and Muslim versions of secular doctrine—and also of democratic, egalitarian, and feminist doctrines.

The feminist scholar Uma Narayan has worked out a theoretical version of these arguments in her book *Dislocating Cultures*. She takes on the charge that demands for gender equality represent "a capitulation to the cultural domination of a colonizing Western culture." As Marx's articles on India show, this charge can also be a boast: all good modern ideas come from the historically advanced countries of the West. It is certainly true that many leaders of the national liberation movements were Westernizers—I have provided enough examples. But Narayan submits two important caveats here, with special reference to what was once called the "woman question." First, when the liberation movements began (in India in the late nineteenth century), gender equality was hardly a dominant ideology in the West, and second, Indian feminists can plausibly argue that their struggle for equality "is no less rooted in our experiences within 'our cultures,' no less 'representative' of our complex and changing reality" than the views of Indians hostile to feminism.[23] Liberation is a reiterative process: it doesn't happen all at once for everybody in the world; it happens again and again. But that doesn't mean that each successive struggle is nothing more than an imitation of the struggle that went before. Yes, many Indian feminists did learn their feminism in the West— remember the Oxford education of Rajkumari Amrit Kaur—but they also made it their own in the course of their engagement with their Indian sisters.

Narayan's book goes well beyond claiming that feminism has Indian roots. She argues for the cultivation of those roots and makes a very strong case for a connected and naturalized feminism—that is, a feminism embedded in national narratives and religious traditions. She helps us understand that liberation is always the liberation of a particular group of people confronting a common history. Let me quote one summary statement of her position, which comes very close to the position I defend in this book.

It would be dangerous for feminists . . . to attempt to challenge prevailing views of "religion" and "religious tradition" purely by resort to "secularism." Many religious traditions are in fact more capacious than fundamentalist adherents allow. Insisting on humane

and inclusive interpretations of religious traditions
might in many contexts be crucial . . . in countering
the deployment of religious discourses [for] problematic nationalist ends.[24]

This isn't an argument about stooping to conquer. Narayan writes movingly about the importance of national
and religious commitments in the everyday life of ordinary
men and women; these commitments shape their sense of
who they are and their understanding of the social world.
She is proposing an honest and compassionate engagement with these men and women. There are pragmatic,
political reasons for such an engagement: refusing it will
"marginalize progressive and feminist voices whose . . .
political interventions into the discourse of nationalism
seem increasingly crucial." But there are also democratic
reasons. Narayan quotes Virginia Woolf's antinationalist
lines from 1938: "As a woman I have no country. As a
woman I want no country. As a woman my country is the
whole world." (Woolf must have been reading Marx on
the working class.) Narayan argues that on the contrary,
women do have a country; they share a fate with their
fellow citizens, who need to hear their voices.[25]

Particular engagements with particular cultures and histories, engagements of the sort Narayan calls for, produce
particular versions of secularism and modernity. Most

militants of national liberation imagined that they were struggling toward a single universal version, with minor variations reflecting national/cultural difference. Their visionary ideal was not different from that of nineteenth-century liberal nationalists like Giuseppe Mazzini, who saw each nation having its distinctive part in the universal orchestra—which would be playing one symphony. Marxists had a more radical singularity in view: the orchestra would consist of individual men and women liberated from both nationality and religion and playing in beautiful, spontaneous harmony. In *Capital*, Marx described a factory operating on the same principle, engaged, of course,, in universal production.[26] But if modern, secular liberation is "negotiated" in each nation, in each religious community, a highly differentiated universe is the necessary outcome. The orchestra might well be cacophonous, requiring negotiations not only within each nation but between and among them, too—but that is a subject for another time.

II

Traditionalist worldviews can't be negated, abolished, or banned; they have to be engaged. I have already made this argument several times. It might not be an argument useful to, or even accessible to, the liberation militants at the height of their struggle against the old religion and the culture of subservience. Only a few intellectuals aimed at engagement in those years, and they didn't get much support. Nehru may have regarded his *Discovery of India* as an example of engagement. What he discovered in Indian history is, impressively, an ancient, complex, and multicultural ("composite") civilization. He even claimed that women fared better in Indian history than in many periods of European history: "Bad as the legal position of women was in ancient India, judged by modern standards, it was far better than in ancient Greece and Rome, in early Christianity, in the Canon Law of medieval Europe, and indeed right up to comparatively modern times." [27] But with regard to the religious traditions that played such a large part in shaping Indian civilization—and in determining the customary roles of women—Nehru was mostly tone deaf. Nor did he have much feeling for the emotional life of his own people, in which religion had a significant role, as did the rich Indian heritage of art and literature. Although he revered the Indian poet Rabindranath Tagore, writes Martha Nussbaum, "he never understood that the liberal state needs public poetry, not just scientific rationality, to sustain itself." [28]

Nehru's discovery (or invention) of a civilization wonderfully attractive to secular intellectuals bears some resemblance to the Zionist discovery (or invention) of biblical

Israel: neither one came to grips with the actual beliefs and practices of the people who had to be liberated. Maybe no such engagement was possible in any of my three cases; maybe the first necessity of liberation was to lay down the secular law, as Nehru and Ambedkar did in the new Indian Constitution and civil code. Only when the new laws turn out to be incompletely effective and provoke a religious reaction do the negotiations have to begin.

The Algerian case suggests that timing may be important here. The efforts of President Chadli Bendjedid to negotiate with the leaders of the Islamic Salvation Front in the late 1980s probably failed not only because of the authoritarian rigidity of the regime but also because of the flaming fervor of the FIS. The Islamists believed that a definitive victory for the one true religion was now within reach. Earlier, in the 1960s, when negotiation and compromise might have been possible, the national liberationists weren't interested; they assigned a distinctly minor role to their Muslim supporters and gave little thought to the principles of Islam. The adoption of the Family Code in 1982 was not so much a negotiation as it was a surrender by the FLN, or at least by the FLN of memory, which only whetted the appetite of its opponents. "This is a front because it confronts," said a leader of the FIS, who promised that if his party won the elections of 1991, there would be no more elections. At that point in the religious revival, negotiation was probably futile; one might well begin to look again for an "Archimedean point."[29]

So the questions that secular liberals and democrats must face are, How could national liberation have made itself central to the ongoing life of the nation? How could it have sustained, how can it regain, its political hegemony? And these questions point to a larger, more general one: What has gone wrong with, what are the obstacles to, the cultural reproduction of the secular democratic left?

Liberation cannot succeed, hegemony cannot be sustained, by negation alone: that is the beginning of an answer to all three questions. "The fact of hegemony," writes Antonio Gramsci, its foremost theorist, "presupposes that one takes into account the interests and tendencies of the groups over which hegemony will be exercised, and it also presupposes a certain equilibrium, that is to say that the hegemonic groups will make some sacrifices."[30] Fierce and unrelenting hostility may be crucial to the liberation movement's initial mobilization, and it necessarily figures in secular responses to the traditionalist counterrevolution, as I have just suggested in the case of Algeria. But it isn't a creative force; it doesn't take the interests of traditional Hindus, Muslims, and Jews into account; and it doesn't move toward the required equilibrium.

Obviously, there isn't a single universal equilibrium. "Taking account" of diverse interests and tendencies is Gramsci's version of what the Indian writers discussed here call "negotiation." Although few of Gramsci's followers have noticed, hegemony as he describes it is not "hegemonic" in the usual strong sense of the word; it suggests dominance, but a compromised dominance, where the dominant group sacrifices some portion of its power, even, presumably, of its principles. This process will produce, exactly as "negotiation" will, different kinds of liberation, different modernities, different secular arrangements. Indeed, I can imagine many different forms of religion-state disentanglement. It simply isn't true, as some early militants believed, that liberation requires the definitive replacement of religion by modern scientific rationality. It certainly requires some kind of religious reform, but it also requires what we might think of as the reform of liberation.

III

Consider now the Zionist case, the case with which I am most engaged. In Israel it seems clear that the negation of exilic Judaism has failed and that the leap to the biblical past and other efforts to find usable bits and pieces of the tradition serve only to produce a Jewish kitsch, which cannot compete with a revived Judaism. The claim to a radical newness gives rise, inexorably, to a radicalized oldness. With Judaism as with Hinduism and Islam, the old oldness may have been more pluralistic, more accepting of difference (in practice if not in doctrine), than either the secular liberationists imagine or the religious zealots admit. Maybe. But I don't think that nostalgia is any more attractive in Israel than in India.

Much needed to be, and still needs to be, negated: the fearfulness and passivity of traditional Judaism, the role of the court Jew, the dominance of the rabbis, the subordination of women. But alongside the ongoing work of negation, the tradition has to be acknowledged and its different parts ingathered, as the poet Bialik argued: collected, translated, incorporated into the culture of the new. Only then can traditional Judaism be pulled apart, its most important features—laws and maxims, ceremonies and practices, historical and fictional narratives—critically appraised. And only then can those features be accepted, or rejected, or revised; only then can they become the subject of ongoing argument and negotiation. It is argument itself, with its varying outcomes, that constitutes the Gramscian equilibrium, not any single or final balance of acceptance and rejection. A person can be a radical critic of the religious tradition, as I would be, while still "taking account" of its value for the Jewish people (or the

Indian or the Algerian people). But the commitment to "take account" means a commitment to learn something about the world of one's opponents. Giving up negation doesn't mean acceptance; it means, again, intellectual and political engagement.

Writing from a religious perspective, David Hartman has made what might be called an equal and opposite argument: that Jewish Orthodoxy must "take account" of the work of liberation and join the "universal struggle to uphold human dignity." That will not happen, he writes, until people who "view the Jewish tradition as the natural context in which to express their concerns" commit themselves to "egalitarianism, human rights, and social justice."[31] A commitment of that sort would be as innovative and revolutionary as any that secular Zionists envisaged; it would produce a revised Jewish law and a very different rabbinical leadership. Hartman's project is one to which Zionist liberation has made a substantial contribution. Perhaps this gift relationship can work both ways. The recognition of tradition as a "natural context" for political engagement is missing in early Zionism (as we have seen); today, I want to argue, its time has come.

Since Zionism is a political movement, the most obvious area for engagement is politics itself. But Zionist negation was first of all a denial that there was a Jewish politics in the exile—or even a collective history. "Since our last national tragedy"—the suppression of the Bar Kochba rebellion in 135 CE—"we have had 'histories' of persecution, of legal discrimination, of the Inquisition and pogroms, of . . . martyrdom," but, wrote Ben-Gurion, "we did not have Jewish history anymore, because [the] history of a people is only what the people create as a whole," and, he insisted, the Jews created nothing in the centuries of exile.[32] In fact, the internal politics of the Jewish Diaspora, through which the people as a whole sustained itself, in scattered communities, without coercive power, for many centuries, is one of the more remarkable stories in the political history of humankind. Exilic politics was in its decadence when the Zionists arrived on the scene, and it had never been valued within the tradition itself. Committed to deference and deferment, dreaming of a distant triumph, the rabbis had little to say about the success of the semiautonomous communities of the Diaspora, and they took no interest in the political lessons that might be drawn from it. This history could have provided an opening for Zionist writers, but they found the decadence of Jewish communal life a more useful subject and made no effort to overcome their ignorance of better days. For some of them, ignorance of exilic history, since it wasn't a "real" national history, was a matter of principle.

Ahad Ha'am at least acknowledged the better days. The sages, he wrote, "succeeded in creating a national body which hung in mid-air, without any foundation on solid earth, and in this body the Hebrew national spirit has had its abode and lived its life for two thousand years." But the true achievement of exilic Jewry–"marvelous and unique," Ahad Ha'am said—was to lose the singularity of "this body" and still survive in scattered fragments, "all living one form of life, and all united despite their local separateness."[33] These fine words were apparently not inspirational; I have not found in the literature of Zionism any discovery of the old Jewish communities, any extended effort to understand how exilic politics worked, or to honor the people who made it work, or to value the achievement. The laws, customs, practices, and implicit understandings that made the communal life of the exile possible— surely this is material for "ingathering," and then for appreciation and critique, by a movement aiming at a new birth of communal life. Indeed, the experience of exile and then of emancipation-in-exile might well teach contemporary Israelis something of great importance: how different Jewish communities could coexist within the framework of a secular state, alongside other forms of difference, other (non-Jewish) religious communities. The new Israeli majority might learn a lot from the experience of the old Jewish minorities.

Another obvious place for engagement, as in India and Algeria, is with the traditional subordination of women, which took different forms in Judaism than it did in Hinduism and in Islam—never reaching, for example, to the radical seclusion of purdah but still banning the participation of women in public religious and political life. The liberationist commitment to create a "new man" was also a commitment to create a "new woman," to free her from her traditionally required submission to patriarchal authority. The actual standing of women in the kibbutz movement, in the Haganah, and then in the Israeli army didn't (and doesn't) always accord with liberationist ideology, but the ideological position is clear: in the new nation-state, there would be gender equality—even, as Herzl predicted, equality in national service. I have already described how religious revival challenges the very idea of equality and how surprised and unprepared the liberationists were for the willingness of many women to return to Orthodoxy and accept a version of the old subordination. They are almost equally surprised by the fierceness of the religious zealots' attack on gender equality wherever it exists—even in the Israeli army, which has been one of the prime instruments of liberationist transformation and something of a sacred cow (to mix my cases) in Israeli politics.

The egalitarian argument will seem obvious to many readers, but simply reciting the argument isn't sufficient. Today religious women in every denomination of Juda-

ism argue for equality in the language of the tradition—
and write wonderfully subtle and intellectually engaging
reinterpretations of both the Bible and the Talmud. It
may be a sign of the polarization produced by secularists
and zealots in Israel that a great deal of the early interpre-
tative work was not done there but in the Diaspora, especially in the United States. Indeed, much of the religious
energy among American Jews today comes from women,
who make up a growing number of scholars in Jewish
studies and, even more important, of ordained rabbis.[34]
Nothing similar is going on in Israel, where secular Jewish women aren't interested in becoming rabbis and religious women wouldn't dream of it (though some, I think,
are beginning to dream).

Perhaps we can see a pattern here. The central office
of Women Living Under Muslim Laws is in London, not
in Algeria or in any Muslim-majority country. Similarly,
many advocates of a "negotiated" Indian national liberation live in the United States. And, although the reasons
are different, many of the Algerian militants who stood
by the original principles of the FLN were, and some still
are, political exiles. Where liberation is incomplete, the
intellectuals and activists who defend it are much like its
original defenders, who also lived for long periods of time
outside the countries they meant to liberate. But arguments for a critical engagement with the tradition will

make their way "home"; they have some chance of appealing to men and women who tire of living with the radical polarity of negation and revival. In all three of my cases, writers and activists are struggling to occupy the space between the poles. In Israel, and, I suspect, in India and Algeria, the clearest examples come from the academic world; the project of critical engagement hasn't yet found what is most necessary to its success: a strong political expression.

I haven't meant to argue that the traditionalist counterrevolution could have been avoided, the paradox of national liberation overcome, had the Zionists, say, fully engaged the tradition from the beginning. But a full-scale engagement early on might have made for a stronger response to the counterrevolution than anything forthcoming today. It might have provided Zionism with a more elaborated, a more interesting, and a more democratic culture. And it might have improved the odds—it might still improve the odds—for the eventual success of Jewish national liberation.

This forward-looking hope suggests a view that has become more and more appealing to me as I have worked on these three cases. National liberation, like every other form of liberation, is a very long process, not a single battle but a series of battles that extends over many decades. Despite the engagement of religious zealots, this process

is secular in two senses of the word (as the dictionary de-
fines it): liberation is a "worldly" process, and it is of "in-
definite duration." It is secular in another sense, too: its
outcome is not determined by faith—not by religious
faith and not by ideology either. The early liberationists
believed that their struggle had a singular and certain end.
But the critical engagement with religious beliefs and
practices is liberating in a new way: now the end is open,
radically uncertain—or, better, there are many different
engagements and many different, always temporary, outcomes. The value and attractiveness of the different outcomes depends on the stamina and energy of the men and
women committed to national liberation. They have to
engage closely with the traditions of their nation while
sustaining at the same time a fierce opposition to all the
versions of traditionalist passivity and oppression.

The task that I've just described has been my own task
in this book. I recommend it to any readers who share my
conviction that many nations, including these three, still
need to be liberated.

Postscript

When I lectured on national liberation at Yale University in 2013, close to half the questions from faculty and students were not about India, Israel, or Algeria; they were about the United States. Wasn't there an American struggle for national liberation (against the same imperial rulers as in India and Israel), and wasn't it followed some thirty years later by an extraordinary religious revival—the Second Great Awakening? And yet the secular state established by the Constitution and its first amendments was never really challenged. Secular political institutions survived and even flourished throughout the revivalist years. Is this another example of American exceptionalism? I will attempt a brief answer to this question by looking for similarities to and differences from twentieth-century liberationist politics.

The differences make up the larger part of the story. Although it might seem to merit the name, the American Revolution is never called a national liberation struggle, nor does it match the model I have been describing. The revolution wasn't a case of national liberation because it involved no ancient nation, living in exile or at home, whose religious culture, partly because of its traditional character and partly in response to foreign oppression, was passive, hierarchical, and deferential. The revolutionaries didn't have to create "new" Americans: the Americans were already new. As Louis Hartz argued long ago, the voyage across the Atlantic was their liberation, or at least the beginning of it.[1] The American colonists did not fit the stereotypes with which twentieth-century Indian, Jewish, and Algerian militants described the people they meant to set free: Americans were not ignorant, superstitious, servile, or fearful. They were free without having gone through a struggle for cultural liberation.

Most Americans were religious, but their religion was also (mostly) new, itself the product of a liberationist movement that developed within and on the fringes of the Protestant Reformation. The idea of religious freedom in a secular state was still a radical and revolutionary doctrine, but it did not require the negation of a long-established orthodox tradition. That tradition, too, was left behind in the Old World. Established churches existed in the colonies, but the establishments were different—Anglican in Virginia, for example, Congregationalist in Massachusetts—and they were precariously established, undermined and weakened before the Revolution by the evangelical revivalism of the First Great Awakening and by what Edmund Burke in his "Speech on Conciliation with the Colonies" called the "dissidence of dissent."[2] Every attempt to create a stable Protestant orthodoxy was thwarted by the fissiparous character of reformed religiosity. The sects created by the Awakening were especially unstable, "subdividing as soon as a member articulated a new, more radical form of spirituality."[3] None of these groups was willing to accept the use of state power on behalf of any of the others, even less so on behalf of the old establishments, so they became the enemies of state-enforced piety.[4] The idea of a secular state did not challenge the deepest convictions or feelings of (most of) the future citizens of the American republic.

I don't mean to suggest that the constitutional separation of church and state was religiously inspired; it was Enlightenment work; its architects, wrote John Adams, were never "in any degree under the inspiration of Heaven."[5] But separation had strong religious support from evangelical Protestants. Writing in defense of Article VI of the Constitution, which banned any religious test for public office, the Baptist minister Isaac Backus made what was a fairly common argument: "Nothing is more evident, both in reason and The Holy Scriptures, than that religion is ever a matter between God and individuals; and, therefore, no man or men can impose any religious test without invading the prerogatives of our Lord Jesus Christ."[6]

As the examples of Adams and Backus make clear, the revolutionaries weren't all working from the same texts or coming from the same place. The political leaders were definitely not evangelical Protestants; some of them were Deists; some of them, we might say, were simply lapsed Christians. (When Alexander Hamilton was asked why there was no mention of God in the preamble to the Constitution, he reportedly replied: "We forgot.")[7] Like many of the liberationists described in this book, the Americans were "Westernizers," although in their case they had to look east to the West; they studied the writers of the French and Scottish enlightenments. But leaders like Jefferson, Adams, Hamilton, and their friends, colleagues, and rivals, made up a fairly thin "rationalistic and skeptical crust" of American society.[8] (The phrase should remind readers of Rajeev Barghava's description of Nehru and the leading Indian Congressmen as the "tiny upper crust that led the national movement.") By contrast, the great majority of the men and women whom T. H. Breen calls "American insurgents" were not Deists, and they were by no means religiously lapsed. Nor were they particularly "enlightened," except with regard to political matters— John Locke was apparently widely read and quoted. Most Americans were pious, even passionate in their piety.[9]

But the opposition that we find in the later national liberation struggles between enlightened intellectuals and militants, on the one hand, and a religious people, on the other, is not visible in the American case. This is explained in part by the religious character of Protestantism, illustrated by Backus's simultaneous defense of the secular Constitution and the prerogatives of Jesus Christ. But it also followed from what we might think of as Protestant sociology. Radical individualism made for separations, splits, and breakaways, and the eventual consequence of continual fissure was the denominational pluralism that distinguishes religion in America from the traditional orthodoxies of India, Israel, and Algeria. Pluralism pressed American Protestants toward toleration, disestablishment, and separation.

Hannah Arendt celebrates the American Revolution because it was, she believes, a political rather than a social revolution—an uprising of disenfranchised citizens rather than of oppressed workers or peasants.[10] She is probably right, although we might argue with her view that the absence of a social revolution is always a cause for celebration. Social and economic inequalities certainly existed in the colonies—in addition to the more radical inequalities between masters and slaves and between men and women, neither of which was at issue in the Revolution (although a number of morally consistent revolutionaries tried to make slavery an issue). Some clerics, especially among the Anglicans, claimed hierarchical privileges, and a sort of colonial aristocracy existed, both landed and mercantile, with wealthy merchants eagerly buying land and setting themselves up as "real" aristocrats. But the colonial elites were a poor imitation of those in the old country, and class divisions were far less profound than in England. Gordon Wood describes the weakness of the American aristocracy: "its relative lack of gentility, its openness to entry, its inability to live up to the classical image of political leadership, and its susceptibility to challenge." Breen concludes that "by the standards of contemporary Europe, white colonists enjoyed remarkable social equality."[11]

Some Americans were nonetheess very rich, and some lived in poverty. Equality was probably more attitudinal than material. But the attitudes were strikingly visible, acted out in everyday life. Colonial aristocrats had short genealogies and little claim on the respect of their fellows. Governor Hutchinson of Massachusetts, for instance, lamented that a "gentleman" did not meet with even "common civility" from his social inferiors. European visitors found Americans unwilling to defer to rank and wealth— irreverent and insolent. In a sense, as Alexis de Tocqueville wrote, Americans were "born equal" as well as free.[12]

This egalitarian sensibility points us toward the most important explanation for the absence of anything like a large-scale social revolution in early American history. In the New World, the revolutionaries had no need to challenge and transform the social consciousness, the everyday culture of (most of) their compatriots. The energy required to leave the old homeland and cross the Atlantic precluded a culture of deference and deferment or of hierarchical submission to priests and aristocrats: everyone had made the crossing. The self-confident activism of the new Americans led to a very harsh engagement with the indigenous peoples of the continent. But it set close limits on the internal harshness of the secular-religious encounter. The weakness of ecclesiastical and socioeconomic hierarchies made anticlerical. and anti-aristocratic politics relatively easy. The anger of later revolutionaries and national liberationists was, not entirely but largely, missing in America.

Arendt attributes that anger, or what she calls revolutionary rage (in the French Revolution, for example), to the politics of "needs and wants." She argues that rage is the "only form in which misfortune can become active."

This is a plausible explanation for mob violence, but not for the authoritarianism that sometimes follows the seizure of state power. It isn't popular rage that is at work here, nor is it the politics of "needs and wants"; it is the political passion and the elitist condescension of a revolutionary vanguard that finds itself at odds, sometimes even at war, with its own people. This war didn't happen in America, and it didn't happen for two reason: because of the "newness" of American society and its religious culture.[13]

I do not want to exaggerate this point. Large numbers of American Tories lived within and defended a culture of hierarchy and deference. Some of them were officials of the crown or Anglican priests, intermediaries of a kind that also appears in the Indian, Jewish, and Algerian cases. A close study of the politics of the Tories and their fate (some eighty thousand left the colonies) might make the American Revolution look more like later revolutionary and liberationist struggles. The Tories were a significant political force in some of the colonies; still, their defeat was something of a sideshow in the politics of the Revolution. Tory marginality is especially clear in what came after independence was won.

The great religious revival in the years after the Revolution fits rather closely the time schedule of my twentieth-century cases: roughly thirty years after the Constitution was ratified, the evangelical uprising reached its height.

But this uprising was not the revival of a traditional culture. It was not a return in militant, politicized form of anything like Tory ideology, it did not aim at the restoration of clerical authority, and it did not challenge the elected rulers and judges of the secular state.

The Second Great Awakening did set off fierce disputes about state-church relations. One of these disputes, about the delivery of mail on Sundays, nicely illustrates what was exceptional about the early American republic. In 1810, the U.S. Congress passed a law requiring that mail be transported and post offices be open seven days a week. The requirement was furiously opposed by many mainstream and some evangelical Protestants as a violation of God's law—a violation especially sinful in what some insisted was a "Christian republic." Sabbatarianism was very strong in the United States in those years. Most states had adopted extensive blue laws restricting commercial activity on Sundays; Congress itself did not meet on that day. But Sunday mail delivery was taken up across the country by anti-Sabbatarians; it became a central issue, with large numbers of evangelical Protestants, especially Baptists, Universalists, Seventh-Day Adventists, and other separatist groups, denying that Congress had any business recognizing a religious day of rest.[14]

Sabbatarian writers and preachers had their own argument from religious freedom: requiring mail delivery on

Sunday, they said, precluded observant Christians from working for the post office. It was the equivalent of a religious test, they said, and therefore unconstitutional. The Sabbatarians were accused by their opponents of planning to establish a single national (Puritan, Calvinist) church, but they probably had no such intention. Some of them were reformers who wanted not only a Christian Sunday but also a day of rest for American workers. Many of the state blue laws exempted groups like the Seventh-Day Adventists (and even the Jews), whose Sabbath was celebrated on Saturday.[15]

In 1828, the mail debate reached the U.S. Senate, which asked for a report from its Committee on the Post Office and Post Roads. The committee was chaired by Richard M. Johnson from Kentucky, a devout Baptist, who delivered the "Report on the Subject of Mails on the Sabbath" in January 1829; it was written with extensive help from Obadiah Brown, minister of Washington, D.C.'s First Baptist Church. It is, as Isaac Kramnick and R. Laurence Moore say, "an amazing document." Any congressional attempt to stop mail delivery on Sunday would be unconstitutional, it declared, for it would establish "the principle that the Legislature was a proper tribunal to determine what are the laws of God." In fact, Congress was a "civil institution, wholly destitute of religious authority."[16]

Johnson and Brown provided an early and passionate

account of the American exception. The rest of the human race, "eight hundred millions of rational human beings, is in religious bondage," they wrote. This "catastrophe of other nations" was a "beacon of awful warning." The authors of the U.S. Constitution had, in response, devised a system of government to guard Americans against the "same evil." The evil was not only bondage but also zealotry. Religious zeal, enlisting the "strongest prejudices of the human mind, . . . excites the worst passions of our nature under the delusive pretext of doing God service."[17] Written by a Baptist senator and a Baptist minister, both of them products of a religious Awakening, that last sentence is itself an explanation for the persisting strength of secularism in the early republic. Neither politicians nor republican citizens, they insisted, have any business trying to serve God; that is the work of individual men and women only. (The Senate report was apparently very popular; seven years later, Johnson was elected vice president, on a ticket with Martin Van Buren.)

The newness of Americans and the radicalism of many American Protestants are probably sufficient explanations for the difference between the American Revolution and later national liberation movements. But another factor, critical because of its absence, seems to me worth considering. The "woman question" did not figure at all in the American Revolution. There was no feminist movement in the colonies, and as Linda Kerber has written, even the most radical American men did not "intend to make a revolution in the status of their wives and sisters."[18] It is also true that race was not a central issue, despite the constitutional debates about the slave trade and the census, and gay rights were as yet unheard of. But the question of gender hierarchy and gender equality is especially important, because of the very strong hierarchical commitments of all the major religions—probably including the eighteenth- and nineteenth-century Protestant denominations except for a few far-out sects (Breen mentions a woman preacher at a Quaker meeting on Long Island, New York, in 1769.)[19] Had there been a revolutionary push for equality between men and women, the religious revival would almost certainly have brought a powerful pushback—which is exactly what happened in India, Israel, and Algeria.

Gender equality wasn't a feature of eighteenth-century liberation, but it is central to all debates about liberation in the twentieth and twenty-first centuries. It is central in the United States, too, and because of this, we are probably less exceptional than we once were. "Religious bondage" is not universal in the rest of the world, as Johnson and Brown claimed it to be in 1829, and it has now acquired some purchase in the United States. Evangelical Protestantism is no longer a radical movement. It is evident here in the United States, as in India, Israel, and Algeria, that something is wrong with the theory of inevitable secularization. But liberation doesn't depend on secularization—or, at least, it doesn't depend on secularization in its most radical version. Today, religious feminists, advocates of gender equality, are at work in all or almost all of America's denominations, and defenders of the secular state and opponents of the idea of a "Christian republic" are active and fairly successful within as well as outside the religious world. Liberation is an ongoing project.

Notes

CHAPTER ONE. THE PARADOX OF NATIONAL LIBERATION

1. Albert Memmi, *The Liberation of the Jew*, trans. Judy Hyun (New York: Viking Press, 1973), 297. See also Mitchell Cohen, "The Zionism of Albert Memmi," *Midstream* (November 1978), 55–59.

2. For a classic statement, see James C. Scott, *Domination and the Arts of Resistance: Hidden Transcripts* (New Haven: Yale University Press, 1990).

3. The hatred of the liberationist militants for every version of ideological accommodation will be illustrated in later chapters. The militant religious revivalists shared this hatred—see, for example, M. S. Golwalkar on Hindu "docility" in *Hindu Nationalism: A Reader*, ed. Christophe Jaffrelot (Princeton, N.J.: Princeton University Press, 2007), 136.

4. Karuna Mantena, "Gandhi's Realism: Means and Ends in Politics" (unpublished manuscript, 2014).

5. Exodus 5:19. Even after the escape from Egypt, the people remain reluctant and frightened. See my *Exodus and Revolution* (New York: Basic Books, 1985), chap. 2.

6. The assassin's immediate motive, he later said, was Gandhi's "pandering to the Muslims." See Ramachandra Guha, *India after Gandhi: The History of the World's Largest Democracy* (New York, HarperCollins, 2007), 38.

7. *Webster's New Collegiate Dictionary* (Springfield, Mass.: G. & C. Merriam, 1980), s.v. "nationalism."

8. Jawaharlal Nehru, *The Discovery of India* (New Delhi: Penguin Books, 2004), 569.

9. For an example from Jewish history, see Gershom Scholem, *The Messianic Idea in Judaism and Other Essays on Jewish Spirituality* (New York: Schocken, 1971), chap. 1, where he gives the classic account of Jewish messianism as a form of political accommodation.

10. V. S. Naipaul, *India: A Wounded Civilization* (New York: Vintage, 1973), 43.

11. Amnon Rubinstein, *The Zionist Dream Revisited: From Herzl to Gush Emunim and Back* (New York: Schocken, 1984), 30. Ben-Gurion wrote this in 1936; for a later statement, see his article "A New Jew Arises in Israel," *Jerusalem Post*, May 13, 1958. See also Oz Almog, *The Sabra: The Creation of the New Jew*, trans. Haim Watzman (Berkeley: University of California Press, 2000).

12. Frantz Fanon, *Studies in a Dying Colonialism*, trans. Haakon Chevalier (New York: Monthly Review Press, 1965), 30, 32.

13. Louis Hartz, "The Nature of Revolution," *Society* (May–June 2005), 57. This is the text of Hartz's testimony to the Senate Foreign Relations Committee in February 1968; it is introduced by Paul Roazen.

14. The maxim originates with Moses Sofer, one of the leading Orthodox rabbis of the nineteenth century.

15. For the text of the manifesto, see Alistair Horne, *A Savage War of Peace: Algeria, 1954–1962* (New York: Viking Press, 1977), 94–95. No principles of Islam are mentioned in it.

16. "Plateforme de la Soummam pour Assurer le Triomphe de la Révolution Algérienne dans la Lutte pour l'Indépendance Nationale," 4. The text can be found on the Internet. For the Cairo compromise, see Ricardo René Laremont, *Islam and the Politics of Resistance in Algeria, 1783–1992* (Trenton, N.J.: Africa World Press, 2000), 119.

17. Horne, *Savage War of Peace*, 469, 133, 316.

18. Mourad Bourbonne, *Les Monts des Genêts* (1962), quoted in Horne, *Savage War of Peace*, 61. Compare Jean-Paul Sartre's line about Fanon: "An ex-native, French-speaking, bends that language to new requirements . . . and speaks to the colonized only." This is exactly wrong; Fanon addresses the French left, where he found his chief readers and admirers. See Frantz Fanon, *The Wretched of the Earth*, trans. Constance Farrington (New York: Grove Press, 1963), 9 (preface).

19. Clifford Geertz, *Islam Observed: Religious Development in Morocco and Indonesia* (Chicago: University of Chicago Press, 1971), 65; Laremont, *Islam and the Politics of Resistance*, 188.

20. "Plateforme de la Soummam," 24. For a (somewhat exaggerated) account of Muslim resistance to French rule since the 1830s and a critique of Fanon for not writing about it, see Fouzi Slisli, "Islam: The Elephant in Fanon's *The Wretched of the Earth*," *Critique: Critical Middle Eastern Studies* 17:1 (Spring 2008), 97–108. Compare B. G. Martin, *Muslim Brotherhoods in 19th Century Africa* (Cambridge: Cambridge University Press, 1976), chap. 2.

21. Nehru, *Discovery of India*, 261.

22. Fanon, *Studies in a Dying Colonialism*, 59n14, 107, 108. For the last quotation, I have adopted Horne's translation in *Savage War of Peace*, 402.

23. Horne, *Savage War of Peace*, 403.

24. Martin Evans and John Phillips, *Algeria: Anger of the Dispossessed* (New Haven: Yale University Press, 2007), 126–38. Compare Fanon's promise: "All these restrictions [on the lives of women] were to be knocked over . . . by the national liberation struggle." *Studies in a Dying Colonialism*, 107.

25. Laremont, *Islam and the Politics of Resistance*, 206; Zahia Smail Salhi, "Algerian Women, Citizenship, and the 'Family Code,'" *Gender and Development* 11:3 (November 2003), 33 (for Salhi and the FIS tract).

26. Gary Jeffrey Jacobsohn, *The Wheel of Law: India's Secularism in Comparative Constitutional Context* (Princeton, N.J.: Princeton University Press, 2003), 95.

27. Shlomo Avineri, ed., *Karl Marx on Colonialism and Modernization* (Garden City, N.Y.: Anchor Books, 1969), 93.

28. Sigmund Freud, *Moses and Monotheism* (New York: Vintage, 2010; originally published in 1939).

29. B. R. Nanda, *Jawaharlal Nehru: Rebel and Statesman* (Delhi: Oxford University Press, 1995), 263.

30. M. R. Masani, *The Communist Party of India: A Short History* (New York: Macmillan, 1954), 24–25.

31. Nanda, *Nehru*, 32.

32. Naipaul, *India*, 159.

33. Horne, *Savage War of Peace*, 133; Fanon, *Studies in a Dying Colonialism*, 160n11.

34. John Dunn, *Modern Revolutions: An Introduction to the Analysis of a Political Phenomenon* (Cambridge: Cambridge University Press, 1972), 161.

35. Geertz, *Islam Observed*, 64.

36. Horne, *Savage War of Peace*, 327.

37. To get some sense of what the left opposition to Congress was like, see Asoka Mehta, "Democracy in the New Nations," *Dissent* 7 (Summer 1960), 271–78.

38. Nehru, *Discovery of India*, 579.

39. Ehud Luz, *Parallels Meet: Religion and Nationalism in the Early Zionist Movement (1882–1904)*, trans. Lenn J. Schramm (Philadelphia: Jewish Publication Society, 1988), 287.

40. Clifford Geertz, *The Interpretation of Cultures* (New York: Basic Books, 1973), 189.

41. Ashis Nandy, "The Twilight of Certitudes: Secularism, Hindu Nationalism, and Other Masks of Deculturation," *Alternatives: Global, Local, Political* 22:2 (April–June 1997), 163.

42. Laremont, *Islam and the Politics of Resistance*, 112.

43. Rajeev Bhargava, *The Promise of India's Secular Democracy* (New Delhi: Oxford University Press, 2010), 253, 261. Compare Ashis Nandy's view: "This is another way of saying that democratization itself has set limits on the secularization of Indian politics." "An Anti-secularist Manifesto," *India International Centre Quarterly* 22:1 (Spring 1995), 42.

44. Devesh Vijay, *Writing Politics: Left Discourses in Contemporary India* (Mumbai: Popular Prakashan, 2004), 157, 158; the author quoted is K. Balagopal.

45. Jacobsohn, *Wheel of Law*, 235.
46. G. Aloysius, *Nationalism without a Nation in India* (New Delhi: Oxford University Press, 1998), 208.
47. Michael Walzer, *The Revolution of the Saints* (Cambridge, Mass.: Harvard University Press, 1965), 177.

CHAPTER TWO. THE PARADOX ILLUSTRATED

1. For the early Zionists, see David Vital, *The Origins of Zionism* (Oxford, U.K.: Clarendon Press, 1975).
2. Jeremiah 29:4–7. This is the New Jewish Publication Society translation; the King James Version has "seek the peace of the city . . . for in the peace thereof shall ye have peace." A very early but prescient account of exilic politics can be found in the book of Esther.
3. Leo Pinsker, *Road to Freedom: Writings and Addresses*, ed. B. Netanyahu (Westport, Conn.: Greenwood Press, 1975), 76.
4. On the deferment of hope, see Gershom Sholem, *The Messianic Idea in Judaism* (New York: Schocken, 1971), chap. 1.
5. Albert Memmi, *The Liberation of the Jew*, trans. Judy Hyun (New York: Viking Press, 1973), 297–98.
6. Theodor Herzl, *Old-New Land ("Altneuland")*, trans. Lotta Levensohn (New York: Bloch, 1941), 79.
7. Shmuel Almog, *Zionism and History: The Rise of a New Jewish Consciousness*, trans. Ina Friedman (New York: St. Martin's Press, 1987), 98, quoting from an article that Herzl wrote in 1899.
8. In discussing the Uganda controversy, I rely heavily on Ehud Luz, *Parallels Meet: Religion and Nationalism in the Early Zionist Movement (1882–1904)*, trans. Lenn J. Schramm (Philadelphia: Jewish Publication Society, 1988), chap. 10 and, on Almog, *Zionism and History*, chap. 4.
9. Vital, *Origins of Zionism*, 138; see also Luz, *Parallels Meet*, 38.
10. Luz, *Parallels Meet*, 271–72.
11. This was commonly asserted at the time by critics of Mizrahi. Luz thinks it plausible but doesn't find enough evidence to say it himself—see *Parallels Meet*, 267–68.
12. Vital, *Origins of Zionism*, 169.

13. For the army and the rabbis, see Theodor Herzl, *The Jewish State*, with an introduction by Louis Lipsky (New York: American Zionist Emergency Council, 1946), 146

14. Some of Bialik's poems help explain why the road was not taken; they express something close to despair about the relevance or value of the tradition. See, for example, "The Talmud Student" in *Selected Poems of Hayyim Nachman Bialik*, ed. Israel Efros (New York: Bloch, 1948; revised ed. 1999), 29–50. The great early effort at cultural ingathering is *The Book of Legends (Sefer Ha-Aggadah)*, ed. Hayim Nahman Bialik and Yehoshua Hana Ravnitsky, trans. William J. Braude (New York: Schocken, 1992); the book was originally published in Hebrew in Odessa in 1908–11.

15. Almog, *Zionism and History*, 121, 199; Ahad Ha'am, "The Transvaluation of Values," in *Nationalism and the Jewish Ethic: Basic Writings of Ahad Ha'am*, ed. Hans Kohn, trans. Leon Simon (New York: Schocken, 1962), 165; Luz, *Parallels Meet*, 88.

16. Almog, *Zionism and History*, 132, 140, 270; Isaiah Berlin, *Personal Impressions*, ed. Henry Hardy (New York: Viking, 1981), 42–44.

17. Haim Hazaz, "The Sermon," in *Israeli Stories*, ed. Joel Blocker (New York: Schocken, 1962), 65.

18. Almog, *Zionism and History*, 134–35.

19. Luz, *Parallels Meet*, 49.

20. Pinsker, *Road to Freedom*, 105.

21. David Hartman, *A Living Covenant: The Innovative Spirit in Traditional Judaism* (New York: Free Press, 1985), 286.

22. Amnon Rubinstein, *The Zionist Dream Revisited: From Herzl to Gush Emunim and Back* (New York: Schocken, 1984), 4.

23. For Ahad Ha'am, see Almog, *Zionism and History*, 87, quoting from an essay written in 1891; the Lenin quotation is from a pamphlet, *How to Organize Competition*, written in 1917 (Moscow: Progress Publishers, 1951), 63.

24. Luz, *Parallels Meet*, 104.

25. Ahad Ha'am, *Nationalism and the Jewish Ethic*, 44–65.

26. On Ahad Ha'am's gradualism, see Steven Zipperstein, *Elusive Prophet: Ahad Ha'am and the Origins of Zionism* (Berkeley: University of California Press, 1993), 77–80, 157.

27. David Ben-Gurion, *From Class to Nation* (1933), quoted in

Shlomo Avineri, *The Making of Modern Zionism: The Intellectual Origins of the Jewish State* (New York: Basic Books, 1981), 200. It is worth noting that Ben-Gurion is speaking here about immigrants from Europe, not from North Africa or Iraq.

28. On the secularism of the early Palestinian militants, see Edward W. Said, *The Question of Palestine* (New York: Vintage, 1989), 164.

29. Danny Rubinstein, *The Mystery of Arafat*, trans. Dan Leon (South Royalton, Vt.: Steerforth Press, 1995), 20.

30. But see Said's warning: "There are numerous possible analogies between Algerian and Palestinian resistance, but ultimately they break down." *Question of Palestine*, 183–84. Some of the analogies, it seems to me, don't break down.

31. Rubinstein, *Zionist Dream Revisited*, 111, 116.

32. Avineri, *Making of Modern Zionism*, 214, quoting from a speech that Ben-Gurion delivered in 1954.

33. The best account of what happened in Israeli religious circles after 1967 is Aviezer Ravitsky, *Messianism, Zionism, and Jewish Religious Radicalism*, trans. Michael Swirsky and Jonathan Chipman (Chicago: University of Chicago Press, 1996); see also Gadi Taub, *The Settlers and the Struggle over the Meaning of Zionism* (New Haven: Yale University Press, 2010); and Gershom Gorenberg, *The Accidental Empire: Israel and the Birth of the Settlements, 1967–1977* (New York: Henry Holt, 2006).

34. Gadi Taub, "Can Democracy and Nationalism Be Understood Apart? The Case of Zionism and Its Critics," *Journal of Israeli History* 26:2 (September 2007), 166–67. Taub is reporting on a book by Motti Karpel, *The Revolution of Faith: The Decline of Zionism and the Rise of the Religious Alternative* (Hebrew), published in 2002.

35. Rubinstein, *Zionist Dream Revisited*, 97.

36. Arthur Hertzberg, ed., *The Zionist Idea* (New York: Harper Torchbooks, 1966), 17–18.

37. Luz, *Parallels Meet*, 170. See also the discussion of Berdi-chevsky in David Biale, *Not in the Heavens: The Tradition of Jewish Secular Thought* (Princeton, N.J.: Princeton University Press, 2011), 152–54.

38. Interview with Gershom Scholem, "Zionism—Dialectic of Continuity and Rebellion," in *Unease in Zion*, ed. Ehud Ben Ezer (New York: Quadrangle, 1974), 277. For David Ben-Gurion's biblical

essays and lectures, see *Ben-Gurion Looks at the Bible*, trans. Jonathan Kolatch (Middle Village, N.Y.: Jonathan David, 1972). Biale points out, rightly, that Ben-Gurion is a "militantly secular" interpreter of the Bible: *Not in the Heavens*, 88.

39. Interview with Scholem, "Zionism," 273.

CHAPTER THREE. THE PARADOX DENIED

1. Yoav Gelber, "Israel's Policy towards Its Arab Minority, 1947–1950," *Israel Affairs* 19:1 (January 2013), 51–81; Ramachandra Guha, *India after Gandhi: The History of the World's Largest Democracy* (New York: HarperCollins, 2007), chap. 4.

2. T. N. Madan, "Secularism in Its Place," in *Secularism and Its Critics*, ed. Rajeev Bhargava (New Delhi: Oxford University Press, 1999), 312–13. Madan would not have been happy with a Leninist Nehru, as the rest of his essay makes clear.

3. Chandra Mallampalli, "Evaluating Marxist and Post-Modernist Responses to Hindu Nationalism during the Eighties and Nineties," *South Asia Research* 19:2 (1999), 171, 173. I am greatly indebted to this article, which helped to shape my own argument.

4. See, for example, Ber Borochov, "The National Question and the Class Struggle" (1905), in *Class Struggle and the Jewish Nation: Selected Essays in Marxist Zionism*, ed. Mitchell Cohen (New Brunswick, N.J.: Transaction Books, 1984), chap. 2 and Cohen's introduction; also Yael Tamir, *Liberal Nationalism* (Princeton, N.J.: Princeton University Press, 1993).

5. Amartya Sen, "Secularism and Its Discontents," in Bhargava, *Secularism and Its Critics*, 461.

6. For a review of the history of the journal and a critique of some of its writers, see Sumit Sarkar, "The Decline of the Subaltern in *Subaltern Studies*," in Sarkar, *Writing Social History* (New Delhi: Oxford University Press, 1997), 82–108.

7. Edward Said, *Culture and Imperialism* (New York: Vintage, 1994), 214.

8. Perry Anderson, "After Nehru," *London Review of Books* 34:15 (2 August 2012), 27.

9. Anderson, "After Nehru," 214. For a specifically Israeli version of this argument, see the work of the philosopher Adi Ophir (in a

series of Hebrew essays), summarized and discussed in David Biale,
Not in the Heavens: The Tradition of Jewish Secular Thought (Princeton,
N.J.: Princeton University Press, 2011), 185–87. Ophir argues that
the "religious-secular dichotomy assumed by nearly everyone to be
the fundamental divide going back to the origins of Zionism is, in
fact, an illusion" (187).

10. Anderson,"After Nehru," 27.

11. B. R. Nanda, *Jawaharlal Nehru: Rebel and Statesman* (Delhi:
Oxford University Press, 1995), 113 (quoting from Malraux's
Antimemoirs).

12. Mallampalli, "Evaluating Responses to Hindu Nationalism,"
188.

13. V. D. Savarkar, *Hindutva* (New Delhi: Hindi Sahitya Sadan,
2003), 84, 92, 113, 126.

14. Mallampalli, "Evaluating Responses to Hindu Nationalism,"
175.

15. For a contrary view, see Shlomo Sand, *The Invention of the
Jewish People*, trans. Yael Lotan (London: Verso, 2009). Sand provides
a specifically Jewish version of a common argument: that the nation
is a nineteenth-century invention. Anthony D. Smith's refutation
of this view in *Nations and Nationalism in a Global Era* (Cambridge,
U.K.: Polity Press, 1995), chap. 2, seems to me persuasive. See also
Anthony D. Smith, *National Identity* (London: Penguin Books, 1991).

16. Guha, *India after Gandhi*, 35. See also the discussion of
Golwalker's ideology in Martha C. Nussbaum, *The Clash Within:
Democracy, Religious Violence, and India's Future* (Cambridge, Mass.:
Belknap/Harvard University Press, 2007), 160–64.

17. Ashis Nandy, "The Demonic and the Seductive in Religious
Nationalism: Vinayak Damodar Savarkar and the Rites of Exorcism
in Secularizing South Asia" (Heidelberg University, South Asia
Institute, Working Paper No. 44, February 2009), 5–6.

18. G. Aloysius, *Nationalism without a Nation in India* (New Delhi:
Oxford University Press, 1997), 181, 185.

19. M. N. Roy, *The Aftermath of Non-cooperation* (London:
Communist Party of Great Britain, 1926), 128; see also Aloysius,
Nationalism without a Nation, 171: "The masses were clamoring for
the demolition of the Brahminical social order, and the upper castes
were struggling to reincarnate it as nationalist ideology through

liberal Western categories." In fact, the clamor was less visible (or audible) than the struggle.

20. Tom Bottomore and Patrick Goode, eds., *Austro-Marxism* (Oxford, U.K.: Clarendon Press, 1978), chap. 3.

21. John Schwarzmantel, *Socialism and the Idea of the Nation* (New York: Harvester Wheatsheaf, 1991), 168; see also 156–58.

22. Otto Bauer, "Socialism and the Principle of Nationality," in Bottomore and Goode, *Austro-Marxism*, 117.

23. David Ben-Gurion sometimes spoke in messianic terms about the return to Zion, but when he was criticized for this by a group of Zionist intellectuals, he insisted that he had a secular view of messianism: it was human work, political work, prolonged and perhaps endless. "We need the messiah," he wrote, "so that he may not come." See Nir Kadar, "David Ben-Gurion's Use of Messianic Language," *Israel Affairs* 19:3 (July 2013), 393–409; for a less sympathetic view of Ben-Gurion's messianism, see Mitchell Cohen, *Zion and State: Nation, Class and the Shaping of Modern Israel* (Oxford, U.K.: Basil Blackwell, 1987), 206–9.

24. Ricardo René Laremont, *Islam and the Politics of Resistance in Algeria, 1783–1992* (Trenton, N.J.: Africa World Press, 2000), 148–49.

25. Thomas Blom Hansen, *The Saffron Wave: Democracy and Hindu Nationalism in Modern India* (Princeton, N.J.: Princeton University Press, 1999), 4–5.

26. Alistair Horne, *A Savage War of Peace: Algeria, 1954–1962* (New York: Viking Press, 1977), 143–46; "Plateforme de la Soummam pour assurer le triomphe de la revolution algerienne dans la lutte pour l'independance nationale," 19–22 (on the European and Jewish minorities). The platform text can be found on the Internet.

27. Martin Evans and John Phillips, *Algeria: Anger of the Dispossessed* (New Haven: Yale University Press, 2007), 122–24.

28. Evans and Phillips, *Algeria*, 154–55, 169–72; Laremont, *Islam and the Politics of Resistance*, 136.

29. Horne, *Savage War of Peace*, 144.

30. For useful accounts of the rise of religious fervor and settler nationalism immediately after the 1967 war, see Gershom Gorenberg, *The Accidental Empire: Israel and the Birth of the Settlements, 1967–1977* (New York: Henry Holt, 2008); and Gadi Taub, *The*

Settlers and the Struggle over the Meaning of Zionism (New Haven: Yale University Press, 2010).

31. Efraim Karsh, *Fabricating Israeli History: The "New Historians"* (London: Frank Cass, 1997), 67.

32. Aditya Nigam, *The Insurrection of Little Selves: The Crisis of Secular Nationalism in India* (New Delhi: Oxford University Press, 2006), 313. Prasad was one of the more conservative Congress leaders. One of Nehru's biographers calls him "prominent in the ranks of medievalism." Guha, *India after Gandhi*, 141.

33. Guha, *India after Gandhi*, 371.

CHAPTER FOUR. THE FUTURE OF NATIONAL LIBERATION

1. Akeel Bilgrami, "Secularism, Nationalism, and Modernity," in *Secularism and Its Critics*, ed. Rajeev Bhargava (New Delhi: Oxford University Press, 1999), 381.

2. Ashis Nandy, "The Politics of Secularism and the Recovery of Religious Toleration," in Bhargava, *Secularism and Its Critics*, 321–44.

3. Bilgrami, "Secularism, Nationalism, and Modernity," 383–84.

4. Nandy, "Politics of Secularism," 335–36, 324. RSS stands for Rashtriya Swayamsevak Sang—Association of National Volunteers. Martha Nussbaum calls the RSS "possibly the most successful fascist movement in any contemporary democracy." See Martha C. Nussbaum, *The Clash Within: Democracy, Religious Violence, and India's Future* (Cambridge, Mass.: Belknap/Harvard University Press, 2007), 155.

5. Uma Narayan, *Dislocating Cultures: Identities, Traditions, and Third World Feminism* (New York: Routledge,1997), 72–73; but see also her stern warning against the idea that "only Westerners are capable of naming and challenging patriarchal atrocities committed against Third World women" (57). I take up Narayan's argument below. For a critique of Nandy's view of sati, see Radhika Desai, *Slouching towards Ayodhya* (New Delhi: Three Essays Press, 2002), 85–89.

6. G. Aloysius, *Nationalism without a Nation in India* (New Delhi: Oxford University Press, 1998), 113.

7. Sumit Sarkar, "Orientalism Revisited: Saidian Frameworks in the Writing of Modern Indian History," *Oxford Literary Review* 16:1–2 (1994), 214.

8. Dipesh Chakrabarty, "Radical Histories and the Question of Enlightenment Rationalism: Some Recent Critiques of *Subaltern Studies*," *Economic and Political Weekly* 30:14 (8 April 1995), 756.

9. Aditya Nigam, *The Insurrection of Little Selves: The Crisis of Secular Nationalism in India* (New Delhi: Oxford University Press, 2006), 60, 73, 310–12.

10. Bilgrami, "Secularism, Nationalism, and Modernity," 394–95.

11. Nigam, *Insurrection of Little Selves*, 320; Bilgami, "Secularism, Nationalism, and Modernity," 400.

12. T. N. Madan, "Secularism in Its Place," in Bhargava, *Secularism and Its Critics*, 311; Nussbaum, *The Clash Within*, 118.

13. Here and in the following paragraphs I rely on Gary Joseph Jacobsohn, *The Wheel of Law: India's Secularism in Comparative Constitutional Context* (Princeton, N.J.: Princeton University Press, 2003), 95–112; and Ramachandra Guha, *India after Gandhi: The History of the World's Largest Democracy* (New York: HarperCollins, 2008), 224–48.

14. Partha Chatterjee, "Secularism and Tolerance," in Bhargava, *Secularism and its Critics*, 360.

15. Jacobsohn, *Wheel of Law*, 98–99.

16. But see Stanley J. Tambiah's acknowledgment that "there was something large-hearted and genuinely accommodative in Nehru's attitude to Muslims in India." Tambiah, "The Crisis of Secularism in India," in Bhargava, *Secularism and Its Critics*, 424.

17. Chatterjee, "Secularism and Tolerance," 361.

18. Harold R. Isaacs, *India's Ex-Untouchables* (New York: Harper and Row, 1974), esp. chaps. 3 and 8. For the most comprehensive account of "compensatory discrimination" in India, see Marc Galanter, *Competing Equalities: Law and the Backward Classes in India* (Berkeley: University of California Press, 1984).

19. See the Web site of the All India Democratic Women's Association. Founded as an organization associated with the Communist Party, AIDWA now describes itself as a part of the independent left.

20. Yoginder Sikand, "Debating Muslim Women and Gender Justice," *Janata* 59:37 (24 October 2004), 9–11.

21. For a description of the work of WLUML, see Madhavi Sunder, "Piercing the Veil," *Yale Law Journal* 112:6 (April 2003),

1433–43. For an account of the organization's work in India, see Asghar Ali Engineer, "Muslim Women and Modern Society," *Janata* 58:47 (14 December 2003), 7–8.

22. Amartya Sen, "Democracy and Its Global Roots: Why Democratization Is Not the Same as Westernization," *New Republic* 229 (6 October 2003), 28–35.

23. Narayan, *Dislocating Cultures*, 17, 30–31.

24. Narayan, *Dislocating Cultures*, 35.

25. Narayan, *Dislocating Cultures*, 37. The Woolf quotation is from *Three Guineas* (1938).

26. *The Living Thoughts of Mazzini*, ed. Ignazio Silone (Westport, Conn.: Greenwood Press, 1972), 55; Karl Marx, *Capital: A Critique of Political Economy*, ed. Frederick Engels (New York: International Publishers, 1967), vol. 3, p. 383.

27. Jawaharlal Nehru, *The Discovery of India* (New Delhi: Penguin Books, 2004), 118.

28. Nussbaum, *The Clash Within*, 119.

29. Ricardo René Laremont, *Islam and the Politics of Resistance in Algeria, 1783–1992* (Trenton, N.J.: Africa World Press, 200), chap. 7; Martin Evans and John Phillips, *Algeria: Anger of the Dispossessed* (New Haven: Yale University Press, 2007), 146–53.

30. Chantal Mouffe, "Hegemony and Ideology in Gramsci," in *Gramsci and Marxist Theory*, ed. Mouffe (London: Routledge and Kegan Paul, 1979), 181.

31. David Hartman, *Israelis and the Jewish Tradition: An Ancient People Debating Its Future* (New Haven: Yale University Press, 2000), 164–65.

32. Amnon Rubinstein, *The Zionist Dream Revisited: From Herzl to Gush Emunim and Back* (New York: Schocken, 1984), 7.

33. Ahad Ha'am, "Flesh and Spirit," in *Nationalism and the Jewish Ethic: Basic Writings of Ahad Ha'am*, ed. Hans Kohn, trans. Leon Simon (New York: Schocken, 1962), 203–4.

34. For the engagement of Jewish women in the academic world, see Lynn Davidman and Shelly Tenenbaum, eds., *Feminist Perspectives on Jewish Studies* (New Haven: Yale University Press, 1994). For three important examples of feminist engagement with the Jewish tradition, see Judith Plaskow, *Standing Again at Sinai: Judaism from a Feminist Perspective* (New York: HarperCollins, 1990); Rachel Adler,

Engendering Judaism: An Inclusive Theology and Ethics (Philadelphia: Jewish Publication Society, 1998): and Judith Hauptman, *Rereading the Rabbis: A Woman's Voice* (Boulder, Colo.: Westview Press, 1998).

POSTSCRIPT

1. Louis Hartz, *The Liberal Tradition in America: An Interpretation of American Political Thought since the Revolution* (New York: Harcourt, Brace and World, 1955), chaps. 2 and 3.

2. *Burke's Politics: Selected Writings and Speeches of Edmund Burke on Reform, Revolution, and War,* ed. Ross J. S. Hoffman and Paul Levack (New York: Alfred A. Knopf, 1959), 71: "But the religion most prevalent in our northern colonies is a refinement on the principle of resistance: it is the dissidence of dissent and the protestantism of the Protestant religion."

3. T. H. Breen, *American Insurgents, American Patriots: The Revolution of the People* (New York, Hill and Wang, 2010), 33.

4. Bernard Bailyn, *The Ideological Origins of the American Revolution* (Cambridge, Mass.: Harvard University Press, 1967), 249.

5. Isaac Kramnick and R. Laurence Moore, *The Godless Constitution: The Case against Religious Correctness* (New York: W. W. Norton, 1996), 41.

6. Kramnick and Moore, *Godless Constitution,* 39–40.

7. Gordon Wood, *The Radicalism of the American Revolution* (New York: Alfred A. Knopf, 1992), 330.

8. Wood, *Radicalism,* 329.

9. Hannah Arendt, in *On Revolution* (New York: Viking Press, 1963), 308n55, claims that "strictly religious influences and movements, including the Great Awakening, had no influence whatsoever on what the men of the Revolution did or thought." This is true only if the "men of the Revolution" were just its intellectual leaders. Compare Breen, *American Insurgents,* 35: "The bundle of ideas, which we associate with such figures as Benjamin Franklin and Thomas Jefferson, did not resonate convincingly with the militiamen who actually turned out to defend communities like Lexington and Concord."

10. Arendt, *On Revolution,* esp. chap. 2. For a contrasting view, see J. Franklin Jameson, *The American Revolution Considered as a Social Movement* (Princeton, N.J.: Princeton University Press, 1967).

11. Wood, *Radicalism,* 121; Breen, *American Insurgents,* 29.

12. Hartz, *Liberal Tradition,* 52–53. Alexis de Tocqueville, *Democracy in America,* trans. Arthur Goldhammer (New York: Library of America, 2004), vol. 2, part 2, chap. 3, p. 589, wrote: "The great advantage of Americans is to have come to democracy without having to endure democratic revolution and to have been born equal rather than become so."

13. Arendt, *On Revolution,* 106. For a critique of Arendt's argument here (and elsewhere), see Benjamin I. Schwartz, "The Religion of Politics: Reflections on the Thought of Hannah Arendt," *Dissent* (March–April, 1970), 144–61.

14. Kramnick and Moore, *Godless Constitution,* chap. 7.

15. For a sympathetic account of the American Sabbatarians, see James R. Rohrer, "Sunday Mails and the Church-State Theme in Jacksonian America," *Journal of the Early Republic* 7 (Spring 1987), 53–74.

16. Kramnick and Moore, *Godless Constitution,* 139.

17. Kramnick and Moore, *Godless Constitution,* 139–40.

18. Linda K. Kerber, *Women of the Republic: Intellect and Ideology in Revolutionary America* (Chapel Hill: University of North Carolina Press, 1980), 9.

19. Breen, *American Insurgents,* 34.

Acknowledgments

This book is a revised and expanded version of the Henry L. Stimson Lectures that I gave at Yale University in April 2013. But it has a long history. I started thinking and writing about the paradox of national liberation in the late 1990s, and in 2001, I contributed an early version of what are now chapters 1 and 2 to a Festschrift for David Hartman: *Judaism and Modernity: The Religious Philosophy of David Hartman*, edited by Jonathan W. Malino (Jerusalem: Shalom Hartman Institute, 2001). In 2005, I gave three lectures on national liberation at the Law School of Northwestern University. I am grateful for the comments I received there from Andrew Koppelman, Charles Taylor, and Bonnie Honig. In 2007, I published a different version of chapters 1 and 2 in the *Journal of Israeli History* 2:2 (September 2007): "Zionism and Judaism: The Paradox of National Liberation." I thought that was the end of the project, but when Ian Shapiro invited me to give the Stimson Lectures, I returned to it and, with his encouragement, completed the lectures and then this book.

Over the years, I have discussed national liberation with many friends and colleagues and have gotten much advice and some criticism, all of it grist for my mill. I want to thank Gur and Dahlia Ofer, Michael Rustin, Brian Knei-paz, Mitchell Cohen, Rajeev Bhargava, Karuna Mantena, Bruce Ackerman, Ian Shapiro, David Bromwich, Steven B. Smith, Joseph Barrett—and Judith Walzer, my closest critic, who points out every pretentious, evasive, ambiguous, or elliptical sentence and demands revision (and usually gets it).

My argument is based mostly on secondary sources, that is, on the work of scholars and journalists who have written about the Indian National Congress, the Zionist movement, the Algerian FLN, and the American Revolution. I have cited their work as punctiliously as I can in the endnotes, but a few of them have had such a large influence on this book that they deserve separate mention here. On India: V. S. Naipaul, Gary Jeffrey Jacobsohn, Uma Narayan, Chandra Mallampalli, Martha Nussbaum, and (again) Rajeev Bhargava. On Zionism: Ehud Luz,

Amnon Rubenstein, Shmuel Almog, and Shlomo Avineri. On Algeria: Alastair Horne. On America: Gordon S. Wood, T. H. Breen, and my old teacher Louis Hartz. But these writers bear no responsibility for what I have done with their work.

As always, I have greatly benefited from the friendship and support of colleagues and staff at the Institute for Advanced Study, perhaps the best place in the world to sit and write. And I am grateful to my friends in the *Dissent* office in New York, who have listened, too often, to many of the arguments in this book. My editors at Yale University Press, William Frucht and Mary Pasti, have provided the same encouragement, tough questions, and helpful advice that I have received from them again and again in the past. I am especially glad that the press is willing to publish a very short book, written in an informal style.

Index

Index

Exceptionalism, American, xiv, 134, 145

Exile, Jewish, xi; negation of the, 38–40, 125, 127; politics of, 37–38, 127–29

Exodus, xii, 4, 8, 33

Family Code (Algeria), 14, 123

Fanon, Frantz, 8, 10, 17–18, 22, 55, 149*n*18, 149*n*20, 149*n*24; on woman's liberation, 13

Fatah, 54–55

Feminism, 119–20, 144–45, 146

Foreign rule: accommodation to, 2, 6, 72; resistance to, 2, 72, 86

Foucault, Michel, 108

Franklin, Benjamin, 160*n*9

Freud, Sigmund, 16

Front of Socialist Forces (FFS), 96–97

Galanter, Marc, 158*n*18

Galbraith, John Kenneth, 17

Gandhi, Mohandas, 3–4, 20–22, 77–78, 105–6; assassination of, 4, 148*n*6; constructive program of, 3

Geertz, Clifford, 12, 22, 25–26

Golwalkar, M. S., 79–81, 147*n*3, 155*n*16

Gorenberg, Gershom, 153*n*33, 156*n*30

Gramsci, Antonio, 124–25

Great Awakening: First, 136; Second, 134, 141–42, 144

Habash, George, 54

Haddad, Waddie, 54

Hadj, Mesali, 27

Haganah, 13, 130

Hamilton, Alexander, 137

Hansen, Thomas Blom, 92

Haredim. See Ultra-Orthodoxy (Jewish)

Hartman, David, 46, 127

Hartz, Louis, 8, 135

Hauptman, Judith, 159*n*34

Hazaz, Haim, 45

Hegemony, theory of, 124–25

Hertzberg, Arthur, 64

Herzl, Theodor, 17, 34–35, 39, 130, 151*n*7; and Uganda, 40–43

Hinduism, 4, 7, 78, 81, 111, 112–13; premodern, 79, 105, 107

Hindutva, 21, 29–31, 78–82, 92, 105–9, 114. *See also* Religious revivalism

Horne, Alastair, 13

Hutchinson, Thomas, 139–40

Indian National Congress, xi, 24, 27, 107, 112

Isaacs, Harold, 113–14

Islam, 12, 53, 91, 97; principles of, 10, 22, 83, 123; radical, 29. *See also* Religious revivalism: Islamic

Islamic Salvation Front (FIS), 15, 123–24

Jabotinsky, Ze'ev, 47

Jameson, J. Franklin, 160*n*10